Advances in Research on Reading Recovery

There is no shortage of innovative educational programs – the challenge is learning how to scale and sustain those with strong evidence of effectiveness. This book focuses on Reading Recovery – one of the few educational innovations that has successfully expanded and established itself in several educational systems in the world. Developed by Marie Clay in New Zealand during the mid-1980s, Reading Recovery is an intensive intervention for young students who are struggling to learn how to read, and has expanded to several countries across the globe over the last 30 years.

Providing evidence of the intervention's effectiveness both in the short- and long-term, this book presents in-depth studies that elucidate why the program is effective, discusses the trials and tribulations in scaling and sustaining the program, and approaches scaling and maintaining from theoretical and practical perspectives. The contributors to this book explain how Reading Recovery has established itself by focusing on evidence and developing a deep sense of community among its practitioners. It has remained at the forefront of effective professional development by offering teachers ongoing and intensive support. Understanding the implementation experiences of the intervention is beneficial for any innovation developer who wishes to grow and sustain an intervention.

The chapters in this book were originally published as articles in the *Journal of Education for Students Placed at Risk*.

Jerome V. D'Agostino is Professor of Quantitative Methods at The Ohio State University, USA. He specializes in measurement and assessment, and the evaluation and implementation of interventions for disadvantaged children and families.

Advances in Research on Reading Recovery

Scaling and Sustaining an Evidence-Based Intervention

Edited by
Jerome V. D'Agostino

LONDON AND NEW YORK

First published 2018
by Routledge
2 Park Square, Milton Park, Abingdon, Oxon, OX14 4RN, UK

and by Routledge
711 Third Avenue, New York, NY 10017, USA

Routledge is an imprint of the Taylor & Francis Group, an informa business

© 2018 Taylor & Francis

All rights reserved. No part of this book may be reprinted or reproduced or utilised in any form or by any electronic, mechanical, or other means, now known or hereafter invented, including photocopying and recording, or in any information storage or retrieval system, without permission in writing from the publishers.

Trademark notice: Product or corporate names may be trademarks or registered trademarks, and are used only for identification and explanation without intent to infringe.

British Library Cataloguing in Publication Data
A catalogue record for this book is available from the British Library

ISBN13: 978-0-8153-8269-0

Typeset in MinionPro
by diacriTech, Chennai

Publisher's Note
The publisher accepts responsibility for any inconsistencies that may have arisen during the conversion of this book from journal articles to book chapters, namely the possible inclusion of journal terminology.

Disclaimer
Every effort has been made to contact copyright holders for their permission to reprint material in this book. The publishers would be grateful to hear from any copyright holder who is not here acknowledged and will undertake to rectify any errors or omissions in future editions of this book.

Contents

Citation Information		vii
Notes on Contributors		ix
	Introduction: Reading Recovery as an Epistemic Community *Donald J. Peurach and Joshua L. Glazer*	1
1	Scaling and Sustaining an Intervention: The Case of Reading Recovery *Emily M. Rodgers*	10
2	An International Meta-Analysis of Reading Recovery *Jerome V. D'Agostino and Sinéad J. Harmey*	29
3	Reading Recovery: Exploring the Effects on First-Graders' Reading Motivation and Achievement *Celeste C. Bates, Jerome V. D'Agostino, Linda Gambrell, and Menglin Xu*	47
4	Getting to Scale: Evidence, Professionalism, and Community *Robert E. Slavin*	60
5	Examining the Sustained Effects of Reading Recovery *Jerome V. D'Agostino, Mary K. Lose, and Robert H. Kelly*	64
6	Differences in the Early Writing Development of Struggling Children Who Beat the Odds and Those Who Did Not *Sinéad J. Harmey and Emily M. Rodgers*	76
	Index	97

Citation Information

The chapters in this book were originally published in the *Journal of Education for Students Placed at Risk (JESPAR)*. When citing this material, please use the original volume number, issue number, date of publication, and page numbering for each article, as follows:

Introduction
Reading Recovery as an Epistemic Community
Donald J. Peurach and Joshua L. Glazer
Journal of Education for Students Placed at Risk (JESPAR), volume 21, issue 1 (2016) pp. 1–9

Chapter 1
Scaling and Sustaining an Intervention: The Case of Reading Recovery
Emily M. Rodgers
Journal of Education for Students Placed at Risk (JESPAR), volume 21, issue 1 (2016) pp. 10–28

Chapter 2
An International Meta-Analysis of Reading Recovery
Jerome V. D'Agostino and Sinéad J. Harmey
Journal of Education for Students Placed at Risk (JESPAR), volume 21, issue 1 (2016) pp. 29–46

Chapter 3
Reading Recovery: Exploring the Effects on First-Graders' Reading Motivation and Achievement
Celeste C. Bates, Jerome V. D'Agostino, Linda Gambrell, and Menglin Xu
Journal of Education for Students Placed at Risk (JESPAR), volume 21, issue 1 (2016) pp. 47–59

Chapter 4
Getting to Scale: Evidence, Professionalism, and Community
Robert E. Slavin
Journal of Education for Students Placed at Risk (JESPAR), volume 21, issue 1 (2016) pp. 60–63

Chapter 5
Examining the Sustained Effects of Reading Recovery
Jerome V. D'Agostino, Mary K. Lose, and Robert H. Kelly
Journal of Education for Students Placed at Risk (JESPAR), volume 22, issue 2 (2017) pp. 116–127

Chapter 6
Differences in the Early Writing Development of Struggling Children Who Beat the Odds and Those Who Did Not
Sinéad J. Harmey and Emily M. Rodgers
Journal of Education for Students Placed at Risk (JESPAR), volume 22, issue 3 (2017) pp. 157–177

For any permission-related enquiries please visit:
http://www.tandfonline.com/page/help/permissions

Notes on Contributors

Celeste C. Bates is Associate Professor at the Department of Education and Human Development, Clemson University, USA. She is also Director of the Clemson University Reading Recovery and Early Literacy Training Center for South Carolina, USA.

Jerome V. D'Agostino is Professor of Quantitative Methods at The Ohio State University, USA. He specializes in measurement and assessment, and the evaluation and implementation of interventions for disadvantaged children and families.

Linda Gambrell is Distinguished Professor of Education at the Department of Education and Human Development, Clemson University, USA.

Joshua L. Glazer is Associate Professor in Education Policy at the Graduate School of Education and Human Development, George Washington University, USA.

Sinéad J. Harmey is Lecturer in Literacy Education, UCL Institute of Education University College London, UK.

Robert H. Kelly is an instructor in the Department of Educational Studies, The Ohio State University, USA.

Mary K. Lose is Professor in the Department of Reading and Language Arts, and Director of the Reading Recovery Center of Michigan at Oakland University in Rochester, USA.

Donald J. Peurach is Associate Professor at the School of Education, University of Michigan, USA.

Emily M. Rodgers is an Associate Professor in the Department of Teaching and Learning, The Ohio State University, USA.

Robert E. Slavin is director of the Center for Research and Reform in Education, Johns Hopkins University, USA.

Menglin Xu is a graduate student in the Department of Educational Studies, The Ohio State University, USA.

INTRODUCTION

Reading Recovery as an Epistemic Community

Donald J. Peurach and Joshua L. Glazer

ABSTRACT
This introduction to the special issue on Reading Recovery situates the enterprise in a broader educational reform context that has placed a priority on developing and fielding large-scale, systemic interventions that support ambitious instructional practice and student outcomes. Within this context, Reading Recovery is examined as an evolving, adaptive *epistemic community* in which tutors, teachers, leaders, coaches, and developers collaborate to produce, use, and refine the practical knowledge needed to support and sustain success among large numbers of struggling readers. Viewing Reading Recovery as an epistemic community provides a framework for more deeply engaging the articles in this special issue, for reflecting on Reading Recovery's history of success, and for speculating about Reading Recovery's future in rapidly evolving policy and reform contexts.

Welcome to this special issue on Reading Recovery, which is among the most established, large-scale early reading interventions in the United States. The articles in this special issue provide perspective on scaling and sustaining the Reading Recovery enterprise; on the effectiveness of Reading Recovery; on sustaining effectiveness; and on the circular role of student motivation in Reading Recovery, both as a dependent and mediating variable.

To introduce this special issue, we begin by situating Reading Recovery in the broader educational reform context in which it emerged and operates. Specifically, we examine policy initiatives that have given rise to large-scale, network-based improvement initiatives (including Reading Recovery); assumptions underlying public and philanthropic support for these initiatives (along with practical challenges that call those assumptions into question); and ways in which networks respond to those challenges.

In putting Reading Recovery in context, we argue that among its most distinguishing (and underappreciated) characteristics is that it is structured as an evolving, adaptive *epistemic community* in which teachers, leaders, coaches, and developers collaborate to produce, use, and refine the practical knowledge needed to support and sustain success among large numbers of struggling readers. That, in turn, provides essential background for understanding and appreciating the subsequent articles in this special issue.

Policy context

Reading Recovery was introduced in the United States in 1984 at The Ohio State University, immediately predating the contemporary standards-based reform movement (Smith & O'Day, 1991). Over almost its entire history, Reading Recovery has operated in a broader educational reform context in which interacting state and federal policy initiatives have sought to hold public schools accountable for supporting all students in mastering increasingly ambitious academic content at increasingly high standards. Couched in the language of "21st century skills" and "deeper learning," the most recent iterations of these policy initiatives attempt to press schools to go beyond a narrow focus on basic facts and skills to supporting students in developing capabilities for complex, authentic analysis and problem solving (Pellegrino & Hilton, 2012, p. 1).

These policy initiatives have also focused attention on supporting teachers in developing the knowledge and capabilities needed to enact much more complex, ambitious instruction (Cohen, 2011; Lampert, Boerst, & Graziani, 2011). In contrast to more didactic, rote instruction, reformers envision more ambitious instruction characterized by ongoing, rigorous assessment and diagnosis of students' capabilities; dynamic design and redesign of instructional tasks; and active adaptation of pedagogical strategies, all while simultaneously managing social dynamics among students. Such instruction is essential not only for addressing the learning needs of individual students but, also, for supporting the development of teachers' professional knowledge and expertise via processes of "pedagogical reasoning and action" (Shulman, 1987, p. 12).

Accountability pressure for ambitious outcomes has been felt especially acutely in early elementary reading, as early reading success is strongly linked to subsequent academic success in other content areas. In both regular classroom instruction and in supplemental instructional venues (e.g., Title I, ESL, and special education classrooms), the aim is for all students, regardless of background, to go beyond demonstrating proficiency in decoding and fluency to demonstrating capabilities to comprehend, synthesize, and critically analyze complex texts.

School improvement networks

Beyond making schools the primary unit of accountability, Reading Recovery emerged and operates in a broader reform context that emphasizes schools as the primary unit of treatment. Indeed, realizing new aims for instruction and student performance requires systemic (rather than targeted) approaches to improvement, in which new designs for learning and teaching are coordinated in coherent ways with complementary designs for (a) the formal and social organization of schools and (b) relationships with family, community, and policy environments.

One approach to systemic school improvement that has enjoyed formidable support is the development of *school improvement networks*. These are networks in which a central, hub organization collaborates with schools and other organizations to develop and field multicomponent designs for addressing schoolwide opportunities, needs, and problems (Peurach & Glazer, 2012).

Networks vary in their goals for improvement and in their scope of intervention, ranging from a focus on specific populations of students (e.g., Reading Recovery) to specific content areas (e.g., Success for All; see Peurach, 2011) to entire schools (e.g., International Baccalaureate; see International Baccalaureate Organization, 2015). Despite such differences, a common feature of leading school improvement networks is a core focus on building educational infrastructure to support teachers and school leaders in learning to work differently, more effectively, and in more coordinated ways toward intended outcomes (Cohen, Peurach, Glazer, Gates, & Goldin, 2014).

The Reading Recovery enterprise takes the form of exactly such a network. In the United States, it currently serves over 3,700 schools and 1,200 districts in 42 states. Functioning as the hub of the network, the Reading Recovery Council of North America and the Reading Recovery center at The Ohio State University collaborate to organize and manage the core programs and services used throughout the network, including publications, annual conferences, advocacy, technical assistance, and special institutes. The network also includes 19 Reading Recovery-certified, university-based training centers that provide support and assistance to both schools and the hub.

Reading Recovery is also among a small group of multicomponent programs that support teachers with systemic designs for identifying and addressing the needs of struggling readers. The program features 12 to 20 weeks of one-on-one, 30-min-per-day tutoring sessions focused on such skills as phonemic awareness, phonics, vocabulary, fluency, comprehension, writing, and oral language. Central to

Reading Recovery is teachers using these tutoring sessions to generate the diagnostic information needed to tailor instruction to students' learning needs. The design of these tutoring sessions is anchored in a uniform framework and well specified set of practices that rest on a set of theoretical propositions as to how children decode and make meaning from text.

Assumptions and challenges

Just as it emerged amidst a press to improve instruction and student outcomes, so, too, has Reading Recovery emerged in a reform context that emphasizes *scalable* interventions (Schneider & McDonald, 2006). Indeed, public and philanthropic support for school improvement networks hinges on their potential to effect fundamental changes in established practices, capabilities, knowledge, and norms in large numbers of schools.

Anchored in a bureaucratic orientation, these networks are widely assumed to support the top-down dissemination of so-called *shrink wrapped*, research-based, and research-validated organizational models that can be implemented quickly and effectively off the shelf by large numbers of schools. This view assumes that a knowledge base supporting expert practice can be developed in hub organizations and then quickly diffused to large numbers of schools.

However, research on leading school improvement networks suggests tremendous difficulty managing school improvement networks as top-down, bureaucratic, diffusion-oriented enterprises. Rather, these networks are often fraught with intractable, compounding problems and puzzles that greatly complicate the unilateral, hub-to-school transfer of a highly developed knowledge base supporting expert practice, especially among large numbers of underperforming schools serving large populations of at-risk students (e.g., Cohen et al., 2014; McDonald, Klein, & Riordan, 2009; Peurach, 2011). These are precisely the types of challenges that complicate rapid, straightforward dissemination of any instructional intervention, including Reading Recovery:

- Uncertainties and inevitable inaccuracies in communicating knowledge of complex practice, as well as the difficulty of teachers and leaders learning to enact and understand their work in new ways;
- The tremendous challenge of diagnosing and addressing the varying and often overwhelming academic and nonacademic needs of students, along with inevitable weaknesses, shortcomings, and flaws in guidance for managing this challenge;
- The tremendous challenge of diagnosing and addressing variability in the initial capabilities of teachers and leaders. Many teachers and leaders in weak schools have modest professional knowledge and skill, are inadequately prepared to enact more complex and challenging practices (and to learn from experience), and require intensive support. Others have more developed professional knowledge and skill and, thus, require fundamentally different (but often equally intensive) support as compared to their weaker colleagues;
- Difficulties funding, organizing, staffing, and managing complex hub organizations and affiliated agencies with capabilities for program development, implementation support, core business operations, and more;
- Uncertainties that arise through collaborations with funding agencies and evaluators that establish constraints on management and on strategic decision making; and
- Weaknesses and turbulence in community, policy, and professional environments, chief among them being a broader educational research enterprise that has struggled to produce a useable knowledge base supporting expert instructional practice.

Learning systems

Thus, the problem for hubs is not one of quickly diffusing a highly developed organizational model but, instead, of *recreating* complex capabilities for practice in many new schools. Reading Recovery is designed to do just that.

Central to the design of Reading Recovery is a three-tiered approach involving collaboration among teachers, teacher leaders, and university-based trainers. To become certified, teachers undergo a year-long, practice-oriented, graduate-level course of study that includes theoretical training, practice, and feedback (Bryk, 2009). With ongoing, practice-based support from colleagues and teacher leaders, teachers continue to develop observational skills and a repertoire of interventions tailored to meet the needs of individual students.

However, research on leading school improvement networks suggests that recreating capabilities for practice in many new schools requires more than a comprehensive approach to professional development (Datnow & Park, 2009; Peurach & Glazer, 2012). This research suggests that realizing and sustaining long-term success depends on hubs managing uncertainty and complexity by structuring their enterprises as dynamic, adaptive learning systems in which hubs, schools, and other agencies collaborate over time to:

- Produce knowledge supporting effective practice,
- Recreate capabilities for coordinated, interdependent practice in new sites, and
- Leverage experience in many diverse sites to refine the practical knowledge base over time.

From this perspective, leading school improvement networks appear to play against type. Rather than instruments of bureaucratic control by hubs, leading networks function as contexts in which teachers, tutors, school leaders, instructional coaches, and program developers collaborate to produce, use, and refine practical knowledge.

Among hubs, schools, and other collaborating agencies, two processes appear key to these organizations learning their way through uncertainty and complexity: *exploration* and *exploitation* (Peurach & Glazer, 2012). Often associated with local adaptation, exploration can be understood as *divergent learning* that involves reconsidering premises, addressing local needs and opportunities, and building ownership and agency through search, discovery, and invention. Often associated with fidelity of implementation, exploitation can be understood as *convergent learning* that involves leveraging established knowledge, selecting from among tested alternatives, and learning and refining through repeated use.

Although reformers have long understood adaptation and fidelity as in tension, researchers have identified large-scale networks in which exploration and exploitation function as *synergistic* learning strategies supporting evolutionary learning over time (Peurach & Glazer, 2012). The process is one of iteratively recreating tested, base-level operations in schools (exploitation); refining and extending capabilities at the school level in response to local needs and problems (exploration); and identifying, selecting, and exploiting favorable program improvements throughout the network.

Epistemic communities

One way to better understand school improvement networks (in general) and Reading Recovery (in particular) as learning systems is to conceptualize them as epistemic communities (Glazer & Peurach, 2015). First introduced by Holzner (1968), the concept of an epistemic community was initially used to examine how occupants of a particular role construct and organize knowledge in a manner that supports common ways of interpreting events and explaining causal relationships.

The epistemic community framework has since been leveraged by organizational theorists to understand the management of knowledge within and across firms (Håkanson, 2007, 2010). As elaborated by Håkanson, high functioning epistemic communities feature an organizational infrastructure consisting of three components, theory, code, and tools, that interact to support the practice, interpretation, communication, and coordination among members of an occupation and across organizational boundaries. As he explains:

> Whether based on the highly tacit knowledge of traditional crafts or on the explicit theories that underlie activities in so-called "science-based" industries, all practice encompasses three fundamental elements: cognitive frames ("theory"), coding schemes and other symbolic means of expression ("code"), and the technology embedded in physical artifacts ("tools"). (Håkanson, 2007, p. 63)

Although similar to community-of-practice models for producing, refining, and using knowledge, the community-of-practice model focuses primarily on social, person-to-person interactions among practitioners working in close proximity (Lave & Wenger, 1991). By contrast, the epistemic community framework focuses on both formal and social mechanisms for managing knowledge, understanding experience, and coordinating practice among professionals locally and in geographically distributed locations.

In that respect, the epistemic community framework is especially useful for understanding Reading Recovery as a learning system: one that goes beyond a comprehensive approach to professional development to engaging teachers, teacher leaders, university-based trainers, and developers as collaborators in an interorganizational, knowledge-producing enterprise that operates not only nationwide but, also, in collaboration with other Reading Recovery networks around the world.

Theory

Theory refers to the accepted set of causal relationships that undergird an epistemic community's problem-solving capacity. Theory, in this context, can entail a scientifically validated set of causal relations. It can also include a set of commonly held understandings, or rules of thumb, about the nature of practice (Glazer & Peurach, 2015; Haas, 1992).

Together, shared understandings about causal relationships among diagnoses and treatments tie together members of epistemic communities and constitute a primary organizing mechanism of professional practice. Supporting the type of exploration central to networks as learning systems, theory serves as a key resource for collaborative problem solving, in that it enables community members to deconstruct and analyze situations that are unfamiliar or are characterized by unexpected results (Patel, Arocha, & Kaufman, 1999). It also situates those experiences in an organizing schema that infuses them with meaning (Håkanson, 2007; Kogut & Zander, 1992). In this way, shared theory creates a common basis for interpreting practice among practitioners who might otherwise arrive at very different conclusions.

Reading Recovery teachers share a common and coherent set of theoretical understandings as to how children learn to read, the nature of the difficulties faced by struggling readers, and the ways in which targeted interventions can strengthen reading skills, all anchored deeply in basic and applied research on early reading (Clay & Cazden, 1990; Pinnell, Lyons, Deford, Bryk, & Seltzer, 1994). These theoretical understandings are supported by a complementary set of ideas regarding how interventions can accelerate the reading of students at risk of falling behind.

The importance of theory in Reading Recovery is not just that it supports expert practice but, also, that it is a central component of an interpretive framework that supports practitioners' collaborative sense-making, interpretation of experience, and analysis of complex or ambiguous scenarios. Shared theory among Reading Recovery teachers supports common interpretation of student reading and writing performance which, in turn, enables a consistent approach to diagnoses and treatment (Pinnell et al., 1994).

Code

Codes are the symbolic means by which community members communicate with each other and their environments. Again, supporting the type of exploration central to networks as learning systems, codes provide visual and written language that supports individuals in explicating tacit understandings, framing their experience, communicating their experiences and observations among each other, and collectively examining and refining understandings drawn from experience (Goodwin, 1994; Latour, 1986).

Code interacts with theory, in that the use of specialized language is what supports an occupation in conceptualizing experience in ways that make it more amenable to (a) diagnosis and treatment and (b) subsequent reflection and ongoing learning. As we have written elsewhere (Glazer & Peurach, 2015), "the interplay between specialized language and shared theory enables organizational members to reflect on and codify experience in ways that enhance performance and build new knowledge" (p. 183).

Reading Recovery entails a highly specified code that supports communication among teachers around problems of practice, such as diagnosing student performance, interpreting assessments, and holding constructive evaluations between trainers and teachers (Bryk, 2009). The most vivid example is the elaborate coding scheme used in conducting an assessment of student reading, which, in the language of Reading Recovery, is referred to as a *running record* (Clay, 2000). The system involves constructing a precise record of a student's reading performance according to specific dimensions that are salient within the Reading Recovery framework. For example, Reading Recovery includes codes indicating a variety of reading behaviors, such as substituting one word for another, omitting a word, student self-correcting, or requesting assistance from the teacher. It also includes distinct codes for interpretation of the running record that signal, for example, how a student uses cues from syntax, visual information, or background knowledge to make meaning from a text.

The Reading Recovery code, then, takes on meaning in its role within the larger system of theory and tools, not only in support of exploration but also in supporting the exploitation and effective use of established, tested methods and procedures. Neither the theory, code, nor tools would, alone, be sufficient to sustain the degree of consistency of practice and interpretation across schools, states, and countries that characterize the Reading Recovery epistemic community. The theory would be of little value absent tools that enable practice, just as practitioners' use of the tools would be greatly limited absent capabilities that enable effective use and the theoretical frame that guides interpretation of experience. It is not surprising, then, that evaluations of Reading Recovery have found a high degree of commonality of practice even in those dimensions of practice that rely on discretion and judgment and are not specified in routines or materials (Pinnell et al., 1994).

Tools

As key resources supporting the exploitation of established, tested practical and theoretical knowledge, tools are artifacts used in practice that increase efficiency, perception, and memory and that aid in the codification, storage, and transmission of articulated knowledge (Håkanson, 2007). Examples include documents, maps, models, heuristics, instruments, and prototypes that are as far-ranging as the expert communities they serve. Tools function as the chief mechanisms in which community members embed and codify essential knowledge of practice and, thus, both retain knowledge in ways independent of individual members of the community and mobilize that knowledge in new sites (Glazer & Peurach, 2015).

Within epistemic communities, tools support the movement of knowledge within and among schools. Once embedded in transferable artifacts, knowledge can cross distances and organizational boundaries with relative ease (Håkanson, 2007; Kogut & Zander, 1992). Further, tools support the coordination of complex work within and among schools, because they make it possible to "chunk, store and communicate technological knowledge" in consistent ways (Håkanson, 2007, p. 75; see also Glazer & Peurach, 2015).

The exploitation of knowledge embedded in tools, in turn, creates the basis for exploration and problem solving. Tools support common experiences among practitioners that facilitate collective reflection and further learning at a level that would be difficult if practice was uncoordinated and idiosyncratic. Further, embedding and codifying practical knowledge in tools functions to make tacit knowledge explicit, thereby exposing personal and parochial theories and assumptions to broader discussion, debate, and verification.

Reading Recovery contains an elaborate set of tools that support and constrain the work of teachers and leaders, and that are common to all members of the network. Some of the key tools include a system of leveled books that allows teachers to match carefully calibrated texts with the specific needs and capabilities of readers; assessment instruments such as the running records template and the observation survey for constructing a diagnostic portrait of a student's reading needs and capabilities, and chalkboard, magnetic letters, writing books, and other materials that support teachers' work with students (Bryk, 2009; Schwartz, 2005).

The epistemic community framework sheds light on the importance of the Reading Recovery tools. For example, the tools constrain and coordinate practice in ways that create a degree of commonality among all Reading Recovery teachers, despite their geographic dispersion. This interorganizational coherence and consistency is the hallmark of an epistemic community, and a characteristic that distinguishes interorganizational epistemic communities from local communities of practice.

Additionally, tools generate common experiences among Reading Recovery teachers that, in turn, create opportunities for the development of shared knowledge. For example, one would expect proficient Reading Recovery teachers to construct similar interpretations of student performance and to make adaptions to practice that were governed by like-minded thinking, despite the variety and subtlety that made these components of practice too hard to embody entirely in explicit routines and materials.

Finally, tools and theory are interactive in the Reading Recovery network. The adaptation of tools to particular situations, as well as the interpretation of their impact on students, depend on a combination of theoretical and tacit knowledge that support sense making across the entire Reading Recovery epistemic community. Bryk (2009) put it well in describing the Reading Recovery system as "a common set of pedagogical practices and materials that are conceptually integrated around a working theory of how students learn to read" (p. 18). Stated otherwise, the tools in the Reading Recovery network create the context for a common set of experiences which, in turn, become the grist for formal and informal learning opportunities, collegial interaction, and collective problem solving.

Thus, in the context of joint work and common practice, tools, in combination with theory and codes, support a dynamic interplay between local and global communities of practice, as well as between the *tacit* and *explicit knowledge* that underly effective performance. Tacit and explicit knowledge are mutually constitutive. Locally developed tacit insights can potentially be codified and embedded in tools, thereby enabling the spread of new knowledge across the epistemic community. The reverse is also true. As new knowledge is introduced into an epistemic community in the form of new tools, it creates opportunities for generating new tacit capabilities and insights derived from the experience of using the tools in practice.

Overview of the special issue

This special issue continues with a collection of articles that provide additional perspective on the design, implementation, and effects of Reading Recovery. Rodgers (2016) provides a comprehensive review of the design of Reading Recovery, examines features of the design critical to scale and sustainability, and discusses experiences evaluating and improving the design in the context of the federal Investing in Innovation program. D'Agostino and Harmey (2016) conduct a meta-analysis of international research on Reading Recovery, with an average overall effect among the highest reported in the What Works Clearinghouse. At the same time, they also identified variability in effects among literacy domains targeted by Reading Recovery. Bates, D'Agostino, Gambrell, and Xu (2016) examine student motivation in Reading Recovery, including the reciprocal relationship between motivation and achievement in struggling readers. Writing from his perspective as a cofounder of Success for All, Slavin (2016) looks across these pieces to further situate Reading Recovery in the context of contemporary educational reform and policy.

It is important to engage each of these articles on its own terms. At the same time, one can see the entire collection of articles as evidence of the possibility of developing and managing novel types of school improvement networks as learning systems and epistemic communities that can evolve and adapt in positive ways in dynamic and demanding environments.

The perspectives of learning systems and epistemic communities are useful for reflecting on the success, scale, and sustainability of Reading Recovery. Further, they are useful for reflecting on the future of Reading Recovery, and on the strengths on which the network can draw in evolving and adapting in response to new policy initiatives such as the reauthorization of the Elementary and Secondary Education Act (US Department of Education, 2015), the Common Core State Standards movement (Supovitz & Spillane, 2015), and the evidence-based reform movement (Slavin, 2005). Finally, they are useful for reflecting on commonalities among Reading Recovery and other leading school improvement networks, most notably Success for All, which bears remarkable similarity to Reading Recovery in organizing and managing its network to support continuous, enterprise-wide learning and improvement (Peurach, 2011; Peurach & Glazer, 2012).

Indeed, as summarized by Pinnell et al. (1994), Reading Recovery founder Marie Clay's "theory of learning to read is based on the idea that children construct cognitive systems to understand the world and language. These cognitive systems develop as 'self-extending systems' that generate further learning" (p. 11). So, too, do the teachers, leaders, coaches, and developers of the Reading Recovery network collaborate as an epistemic community to support struggling students in learning to read. Viewed from this perspective, Reading Recovery functions as the self-extending cognitive system through which their understandings and practice evolve in response to students, their own work, and the broader environments in which both are situated.

References

Bates, C. C., D'Agostino, J. V., Gambrell, L., & Xu, M. (2016). Reading Recovery: Exploring the effects on first-graders' reading motivation and achievement. *Journal of Education for Students Placed At Risk, 21,* 47–59.

Bryk, A. S. (2009). Reflections from a two-decade association with Reading Recovery. *Journal of Reading Recovery, 9,* 17–19.

Clay, M. M. (2000). *Running records for classroom teachers.* Portsmouth, NH: Heinemann.

Clay, M. M., & Cazden, C. B. (1990). A Vygotskian interpretation of Reading Recovery. In L. C. Moll (Ed.), *Vygotsky and education: Instructional implications and applications of sociohistorical psychology* (pp. 206–222). New York, NY: Cambridge University Press.

Cohen, D. K. (2011). *Teaching and its predicaments.* Cambridge, MA: Harvard University Press.

Cohen, D. K., Peurach, D. J., Glazer, J. L., Gates, K. E., & Goldin, S. (2014). *Improvement by design: The promise of better schools.* Chicago, IL: University of Chicago Press.

D'Agostino, J. V., & Harmey, S. J. (2016). An international meta-analysis of Reading Recovery. *Journal of Education for Students Placed At Risk, 21,* 29–46.

Datnow, A., & Park, V. (2009). Towards the co-construction of educational policy: Large-scale reform in an era of complexity. In D. Plank, B. Schneider, & G. Sykes (Eds.), *Handbook of education policy research* (pp. 348–361). New York, NY: Routledge.

Glazer, J. L., & Peurach, D. J. (2015). Occupational control in education: The logic and leverage of epistemic communities. *Harvard Educational Review, 85,* 172–202.

Goodwin, C. (1994). Professional vision. *American Anthropologist, 96,* 606–633.

Haas, P. (1992). Introduction: Epistemic communities and international policy coordination. *International Organization, 46,* 1–35.

Håkanson, L. (2007). Creating knowledge: The power and logic of articulation. *Industrial and Corporate Change, 16*(1), 51–88.

Håkanson, L. (2010). The firm as an epistemic community: The knowledge-based view revisited. *Industrial and Corporate Change, 19,* 1801–1828.

Holzner, B. (1968). *Reality construction in society.* Cambridge, MA: Schenkman.

International Baccalaureate Organization. (2015). *Education for a better world.* Bethesda, MD: IB Global Centre.

Kogut, B., & Zander, U. (1992). Knowledge of the firm, combinative capabilities, and the replication of technology. *Organization Science, 3,* 383–397.

Lampert, M., Boerst, T. A., & Graziani, F. (2011). Organizational resources in the service of school-wide ambitious teaching practice. *Teachers College Record, 113,* 1361–1400.

Latour, B. (1986). Visualization and cognition. *Knowledge and Society, 6,* 1–40.

Lave, J., & Wenger, E. (1991). *Situated learning: Legitimate peripheral participation.* London, UK: Cambridge University Press.

McDonald, J. P., Klein, E. J., & Riordan, M. (2009). *Going to scale with new schools designs: Reinventing high schools.* New York, NY: Teachers College Press.

Patel, V. L., Arocha, J. F., & Kaufman, D. R. (1999). Expertise and tacit knowledge in medicine. In R. J. Sternberg & J. R. Horvath (Eds.), *Tacit knowledge in professional practice* (pp. 75–100). Hillsdale, NJ: Lawrence Erlbaum.

Pellegrino, J. W., & Hilton, M. L. (Eds.) (2012). *Education for life and work: Developing transferable knowledge and skills in the 21st century.* Washington, DC: National Academies Press.

Peurach, D. J. (2011). *Seeing complexity in public education: Problems, possibilities, and Success for All.* New York, NY: Oxford University Press.

Peurach, D. J., & Glazer, J. L. (2012). Reconsidering replication: New perspectives on large-scale school improvement. *Journal of Educational Change, 13,* 155–190.

Pinnell, G. S., Lyons, C. A., Deford, D. E., Bryk, A. S., & Seltzer, M. (1994). Comparing instructional models for the literacy education of high-risk first graders. *Reading Research Quarterly, 29*, 8–39.

Rodgers, E. (2016). Scaling and sustaining an intervention: The case of Reading Recovery. *Journal of Education for Students Placed At Risk, 21*, 10–28.

Schneider, B., & McDonald, S. K. (Eds.). (2006). *Scale up in education: Volume I—Ideas in principle*. Lanham, MD: Rowman & Littlefield.

Schwartz, R. M. (2005). Literacy learning of at-risk first-grade students in the Reading Recovery Early Intervention. *Journal of Educational Psychology, 97*, 257–267.

Shulman, L. S. (1987). Knowledge and teaching: Foundations of the new reform. *Harvard Education Review, 57*, 1–22.

Slavin, R. E. (2005). *Evidence-based reform: Advancing the education of students at risk*. Washington, DC: Center for American Progress.

Slavin, R. E. (2016). Getting to Scale: Evidence, Professionalism, and Community. *Journal of Education for Students Placed At Risk, 21*, 60–63.

Smith, M. S., & O'Day, J. (1991). Systemic school reform. In S. H. Fuhrman & B. Malen, (Eds.), *The politics of curriculum and testing: The 1990 Yearbook of the Politics of Education Association* (pp. 233–267). New York, NY: Falmer.

Supovitz, J. A., & Spillane, J. P. (Eds.) (2015). *Challenging standards: Navigating conflict and building capacity in the era of the Common Core*. Lanham, MD: Rowman & Littlefield.

U.S. Department of Education. (2015). *Elementary and Secondary Education Act*. Retrieved October 5, 2015 from http://www.ed.gov/esea.

Scaling and Sustaining an Intervention: The Case of Reading Recovery

Emily M. Rodgers

> **ABSTRACT**
> In every school district across the country, every year, initiatives are adopted with the goal of improving the literacy performance of young students, and, just as frequently, these initiatives fail or quickly become passing fads. In this article, Rodgers reviews literature related to scaling educational innovations and describes challenges and barriers to implementing and maintaining evidence-based reform. Using Reading Recovery as a case example, she describes features of the intervention that are thought to be linked to its longevity in terms of scalability and sustainability. She also shares lessons learned from the most recent period of its expansion with the 5-year grant to scale up Reading Recovery across the county. Implications from this article include the importance of adopting an initiative that has a well-articulated design, collecting data on the progress of the students served, and having a person in the district who acts as a redirecting agent, maintaining the design of the initiative and guarding it against tendencies to pare down the design.

Six national reading reports over the last 3 decades and the ongoing review work of the U.S. Department of Education's What Works Clearinghouse have yielded an abundance of evidence about effective instructional practices, particularly for young students having great difficulty learning to read and write. Despite this growing body of knowledge, however, a persistent problem remains: how to bring evidence-based practices to scale (Denton, Vaughn, & Fletcher, 2003).

In this article, I review literature related to scaling educational innovations and describe challenges and barriers to implementing and sustaining evidence-based reform. Using Reading Recovery as a case example, I describe features of the intervention that seem to be linked to its longevity in terms of scalability and sustainability. Implications from this article include the importance of adopting an initiative that has a well-articulated design, collecting data on the progress of the students served, and having a person in the district who acts as a *redirecting agent* (Clay, 1994), maintaining the design of the initiative and guarding the design against tendencies to pare it down for something inferior.

What does it mean to scale an innovation in education?

Coburn (2003) maintained that the concept of scaling an innovation is much more nuanced than simply increasing the number of schools in which an innovation is implemented. Stringfield and Datnow (1998) made the same point 15 years earlier when they described what was at the time a new trend in educational policy and research: finding ways to bring school-improvement designs to scale. There had been an increase in federal funding to support comprehensive school-reform models, and, according to Stringfield and Datnow, attention had shifted to finding ways to bring these successful designs to scale. It was within that context of whole school improvement that Stringfield and Datnow defined scaling up as "the deliberate expansion to many settings of an externally developed school-restructuring design that previously has been used successfully in one or a small number of school settings" (p. 271).

Schneider and MacDonald's (2007) definition of scaling goes beyond the idea of increasing the number of schools taking up an innovation. They emphasize two features in their definition: enacting an already proven intervention in a different context (one that is larger and more diverse than its original context) and maintaining positive impact as it is enacted in these new contexts. From this perspective, then, replicating an innovation in more and more schools that are no different from the original context would not be regarded as scaling an innovation. Further, if results cannot be maintained in the new contexts, the innovation has not scaled.

Coburn (2003) conceptualized scale as having four dimensions: depth, sustainability, spread, and shift in ownership. By depth, Coburn meant that to be at scale, the innovation must have created deep change, going beyond simple surface changes (such as changing materials or how the school day is organized) to changing teachers' beliefs and the pedagogical principles embodied in the curriculum. Sustainability, which Coburn identified as perhaps the fundamental element of scale, refers to whether an innovation is maintained over time in the schools in which it is implemented or dropped after a short period of use. Spread, the third feature of Coburn's conceptualization of scale, refers not only to an innovation spreading to other schools (breadth of scale) but, also, to whether and how the innovation (in terms of its norms, practices, and beliefs) spreads within schools to other classrooms (depth of scale). Finally, Coburn described an innovation as having scaled if the reform shifts to becoming regarded as an internal reform, no longer as an external one brought in by someone outside the school; at this point, the innovation is regarded as belonging to the school or system.

Taken together, these definitions of scaling, and of what it means to be at scale, present a challenge to developers of new educational initiatives who want to take their innovation to scale. The definitions suggest that, to scale, an innovation must not only expand to more schools, but to different kinds of schools, all the while maintaining its effectiveness; that the impact of the innovation should be wide and deep across the settings where it is implemented; and that the ultimate goal of the innovation is that it shifts from being viewed as an external initiative to one that is locally owned.

Perspectives on the success and failure of innovations to scale

In every school district across the country, each year, new initiatives are adopted with the goal of improving the literacy performance of young students. Just as frequently, these initiatives fail or quickly become passing fads. Elmore (1996) summed up this problem of scale with the statement: "Innovations that require large changes in the core of educational practice seldom penetrate more than a fraction of US schools and classrooms, and seldom last long when they do" (p. 2). Various perspectives exist as to why educational innovations scale or fail.

Why innovations succeed and scale

Datnow and Stringfield's (2000) review of data from 16 school-reform-focused studies provides a helpful framework to understand better what it takes to bring lasting change to a school. A key feature, they concluded, in implementing and sustaining a reform initiative is that groups of stakeholders, at the state, district, and local levels, work together in an integrated way, rather than a few individuals working in isolation from others who also are involved in the setting.

Slavin and Madden (2007) also underscored the importance of a network, but their approach differs in terms of its composition. Drawing on lessons learned from their scaling-up of Success for All (SFA), Slavin and Madden advocate creating two networks of stakeholders that go beyond the school setting and are created principally to provide support to the other members in the network: a network of other schools prepared to help new schools implement the innovation, and a network of a core group of trainers who coordinate between the project's headquarters and the regional training sites. Members in the network all share the same goal, implementing and sustaining the SFA model in schools; they do not have competing agendas or other stakeholders lobbying for their resources, time, or funding in the way that state legislators or district administrators do. The advantage of a network beyond the local context is that the innovation can be somewhat sheltered against the policy changes that invariably accompany changes of school and district administrators.

Slavin and Madden (2007) identified several other features necessary for an innovation to scale, features that match well with the definitions of scaling discussed in the previous section. They noted that the quality of the innovation must be maintainable as the innovation spreads, it should have a strong research base to continually investigate and demonstrate the innovation's effectiveness, and it should provide specified procedures and materials to the school to ease the uptake of the new instructional approach.

Gersten, Chard, and Baker (2000), focusing on factors that affect the sustained use of evidence-based core teaching practices, noted the importance of teachers becoming skilled with the teaching order for an innovation to be scaled. When teachers have a deeper conceptual understanding of the instructional practice, there is a greater likelihood, they argued, that teachers will continue to implement the instructional practice, even after incentives are removed or disappear. This idea of working toward a deeper conceptual understanding of the new practice also fits with Fullan's (1993) observation that change cannot be mandated, not when the nature of change requires skillful thinking and decision-making.

Guskey's (1986) finding, that changes in teacher beliefs and motivation only come after changes in practice, suggests that, to achieve the deeper conceptual change that Gersten and colleagues (2000) and Fullan (1993) argued for, the teacher should be engaged in the new practice from the outset of adopting the innovation. In other words, the way to deep change is not through discussion, but through taking on the new instruction. Beliefs will change after the teacher sees the effects of the new program on student learning and not as a result of prolonged discussions about theory.

Why innovations fail and disappear

Stringfield and Datnow (1998) proposed that programs fail to expand because of flaws with the program's design. On the one hand, they argued, programs may fail to scale simply because they do not really work. Instead, they only appear to work because they rely on "heroic efforts by individuals who are extraordinarily talented and dedicated. As the programs are taken to scale, less heroic leaders are unable to use the practices to improve the academic achievements of students" (p. 270). Alternatively, Stringfield and Datnow proposed that, if it is the case that programs actually do work, the inability to scale is likely due to some flaw with the program's design, and that the developers did not build it in ways for the program to be taken up in different settings from its original site. In both scenarios, the problem lies within the design of the innovation. They emphasized that, for effective scaling up to occur, there would need to be a way for the innovation's design to develop and change as the number of schools implementing it increases.

In their literature review, Cohen and Ball (2007) differentiated between problems with the design and problems with the educational system itself. Those who fault the innovation, according to Cohen & Ball's review, cite issues with the program's design or argue that the innovation did not address important, critical issues to the system. On the other hand, those who identify the education system as the reason for innovation failure argued that there is a lack of incentive for change, or that the educational environment is so complex and fragmented that consistency of adoption is inhibited from one school to another.

Wilson and Daviss (1994) took the first perspective identified by Cohen and Ball (2007), that innovations fail when they are poorly designed. Failed innovations, Wilson and Daviss argued, represent a piecemeal approach to change rather than a design. Having a design means that the innovation has built-in mechanisms to accomplish two seemingly opposing actions: one, to enable change to occur to the innovation as research warrants the change, and, two, to keep the innovation the same from place to place—in other words, maintain fidelity to the innovation. Without a design, the innovation cannot be replicated with good fidelity and scaled beyond the local educational setting where it was initially developed.

Petroski (2006) wrote about the role of design in engineering, but his ideas are relevant for education. He noted that once a design is known to work, there is a press to change it, especially with respect to identifying materials that might be superfluous and so can be eliminated, usually to save costs. Fullan (1993) identified this tension in education, too: the press to keep the status quo and not change instructional practices, matched against the press to change and do something differently. This tension needs to be managed, and good designs needed to be guarded against unwarranted change; if not, good designs can be weakened so much so that they lose their effectiveness. As Petroski warned, "The cumulative effect of such paring down of strength is a product that can more readily fail. If the trend continues indefinitely, failure is sure to occur" (2001, p. 171).

In the sections that follow, I turn to the case of Reading Recovery, a literacy intervention for first-grade students, to provide an example of an educational innovation that appears to be beating the odds and scaling up. Reading Recovery's design and implementation pattern to date are outlined and compared to the features of scaling described in the previous section. I then use Reading Recovery's case to offer a fresh synthesis of what it means to scale an educational innovation.

Scaling an innovation: The case of Reading Recovery

The overarching goal of Reading Recovery is to provide intensive, long-term professional development for teachers so they can design and deliver one-to-one, short-term, 30-min lessons each day to first-grade students having the greatest difficulty learning to read and write. Students are identified for Reading Recovery through a standard selection protocol. Typically, the lower one third of a first-grade cohort is selected for initial screening. These low achieving children are assessed with the tool, *An Observation Survey of Early Literacy Achievement* (Clay, 2013), the National Center on Response to Intervention's (NCRTI) highest rated screening instrument for beginning reading difficulties (D'Agostino, 2012; NCRTI, 2014). The lowest achieving students are then selected for Reading Recovery lessons.

The rationale for early identification and intervention is twofold. Children can be identified as falling behind their peers in terms of literacy development after just one year at school. If then provided a short-term, intensive literacy intervention at the first sign of reading difficulties, these children may be able to recover their progress and catch up to their peers. There are two positive outcomes from intervening early with instruction that is more intensive than what can be offered in the classroom: Children either respond quickly and catch up to their peers within 20 weeks or, if they do not respond well, they can be more reliably referred for assessment and possible placement in special education.

Reading Recovery was piloted in six schools in one school district in Columbus, Ohio, in 1984–1985. Thirty years later, that first implementation of Reading Recovery in the United States at Ohio State, with its trademark network of three-tiered, embedded professional development involving university, school district, and school collaboration, has been replicated at over 20 other universities in the country.

Reading Recovery's design

Reading Recovery's design includes six critical features: three-tiered, job-embedded professional development to create expert teachers, a network of professional support for the stakeholders involved, an established instructional format and materials for teaching children, a research and evaluation system, published standards which articulate the details of these features, and a mechanism for redesign (Rodgers, 2002, 2012). These six features have evolved and were refined throughout the course of Reading Recovery's development and validation in the United States.

Three-tiered job-embedded professional development

Reading Recovery's professional development design reorganizes and introduces new structures to the system. These structures enable the district to implement the changes and carry them forward more independently without needing continued close involvement of the university (Clay, 1994).

At one tier of professional development, teachers complete two graduate courses offered by district-level teacher leaders to learn how to assess literacy achievement and design and deliver Reading Recovery lessons. After the initial training, teachers continue to participate in ongoing professional development offered by the teacher leaders. Teachers typically work in the Reading Recovery role for 2.5 hr a day and in some other instructional role during the rest of the day, most often as classroom teacher or Title I teacher working with small reading groups.

Teacher-leader training, the next tier of professional development, is postgraduate work. Teacher leaders complete 15 post-Masters hr at an accredited Reading Recovery University Training Center to prepare them to be expert teachers of children and coaches for teachers. Teacher leaders study theory related to reading difficulties and learn how to support teachers in cases where children are not making expected progress in the intervention.

Teacher-leader training is provided by trainers, either faculty or staff members, at the university. At this third tier, trainers participate in a year-long postdoctoral mentorship experience at one of the two universities in the United States that provide trainer training. Their training prepares them to direct a university training site at their home institutions and offer the course work and ongoing professional development for teacher leaders.

In sum, university-level trainers provide training and professional development to teacher leaders who work in school districts to provide training and ongoing coaching to teachers who provide Reading Recovery lessons to first graders in schools. Trainers, teachers, and teacher leaders start teaching Reading Recovery lessons while they are taking the coursework; in other words, they start teaching children Reading Recovery lessons right away, rather than waiting until after they have completed the training. The rationale is twofold: No student instructional time is lost waiting for teachers to finish their coursework, and teachers have a more supportive learning environment in which to learn how to assess and make instructional decisions as they teach students. As such, Reading Recovery training is a good example of job-embedded professional development.

An instructional format and materials for teaching children

Reading Recovery lessons are 30 min long and provided daily in a one-to-one instructional setting. Each lesson is comprised of six components: instruction in fluent and phrased reading, assessment of independent oral reading, isolated word work to learn word identification strategies, letter work to build letter identification and recognition, composing and writing a short message, and reading a new book with the teacher's help. Although the lesson components are the same for each lesson, the lessons are not scripted, and teachers must learn how to prompt for and teach students to read and write increasingly more complex text with more and more independence. Syllabi may vary across university centers, but common texts are used to learn how to design and deliver Reading Recovery lessons. In addition, teachers select books for instruction from a common list that contains titles from multiple publishers, all titles selected, reviewed, field tested, and assigned a difficulty level by a committee of Reading Recovery professionals.

A research and evaluation system

Data are collected on each student served by Reading Recovery, as well as a comparison group, in accordance with a standard evaluation protocol. A center was established at Ohio State very early on to collect these data and provide annual school-, district-, state-, and national-level reports. These annual evaluation reports follow a standard protocol that includes information about teacher and student demographics and students' progress on standard literacy measures. Data as to the length of time in the program, schools' level of implementation, teacher and student absenteeism, and their relationship to outcomes are also provided.

Networks of professional support

A regional teacher-training site is a new entity within the educational organization; it provides the structure at a district- or cross-district level to provide professional development to the teachers. Several districts may form a consortium to support the costs related to having a teacher leader and a regional training site. The site is usually located at an already existing professional-development space within the school district that acts as the fiscal agent for the site. The training site contains a one-way mirror to observe lessons and space for teachers to have a class meeting. Each regional teacher-training site is affiliated with a university training center.

In addition to the local network of support that is provided by the regional teacher-training site, teachers have access to a national network as well through the Reading Recovery Council of North America (RRCNA), a not-for-profit association of Reading Recovery professionals, advocates, and partners. The Council provides a network of opportunities for leadership and professional development and a wide variety of programs and services, including publications, annual conferences, advocacy, technical assistance, and special institutes. These activities strengthen the implementation of Reading Recovery and provide opportunities for Reading Recovery professionals to collaborate with early-literacy advocates and other education professionals.

Published standards

Consistent with Cohen and Ball's (2007) recommendation that new professional norms be developed to support the implementation of new instructional practices, Reading Recovery's period of development and validation in the United States has included the development of common professional standards, *Standards and Guidelines of Reading Recovery in the United States, 6th edition* (RRCNA, 2014). The standards describe norms for operating a regional training site, and the roles and responsibilities of teachers, teacher leaders and trainers, and site coordinators. A royalty-free license is issued annually to each regional teacher-training site on the basis of meeting the standards. Standards and the issuance of annual site licenses ensure the internal and external fidelity of Reading Recovery implementation.

A mechanism for redesigning

The license for Reading Recovery in the United States is owned by The Ohio State University. It issues the annual, royalty-free licenses to universities and teacher training sites as long as the individuals at these sites follow the standards. Changes to the standards are made through discussion and consensus amongst the national group of Reading Recovery university trainers, called the North American Trainer Group. This group meets twice yearly to discuss training, implementation, evaluation, and research issues connected to the program.

There is a constant press for change to Reading Recovery and the impetus for change often arises from the feedback loop provided by the annual evaluation reports or requests for waivers to standards. Two examples of press for change and how they were managed include the use of technology in training and the one-to-one nature of student instruction.

In the first example, pressure for change came from the implementation of the scale-up grant. With its emphasis on reaching teachers in rural areas, the grant added pressure for redesign to the program's traditional face-to-face training for teachers. Several studies were undertaken at multiple universities using varying formats of both face-to-face training and training by distance models to determine how the infusion of technology might affect the effectiveness of the program (D'Agostino & Rodgers, 2015). Results have been positive and discussed by the trainer group, and now the national standard design for teacher training is evolving to incorporate the use of distance learning. These changes will be reflected in a new edition of standards for Reading Recovery currently being revised.

There is also constant pressure to change the one-to-one feature of Reading Recovery's design for children. Multiple studies of one-to-one versus small-group instruction have as yet failed to demonstrate the effect sizes that are achieved with individualized instruction (see Brown, Morris, & Fields, 2005; D'Agostino & Murphy, 2004; Schwartz, 2005). As a result, the intervention has not changed to a small-group format, despite the pressure to change. In this case, the pressure to change the design might be best characterized as a pressure to substitute an inferior ingredient for the sake of cost.

These two examples of pressure for change, one in which change is occurring and the other where no change has been made, demonstrate that Reading Recovery has a mechanism for considering redesign. The structure of the national network of trainers allows for ongoing consideration of changing the intervention.

Summary: Reading Recovery's design

Reading Recovery has a clearly articulated design, and the design itself incorporates features identified in the literature as critical for scaling up: specified core materials for instruction, an emphasis on creating expert, skilled teachers, a professional network beyond the local context, and a way for the design to change. These features are all clearly described in a document that identifies standards associated with the innovation, and these are maintained each year by the issuing of royalty-free license letters to sites and universities that uphold the standards. In these ways, the innovation can be assured not only of fidelity of its design but also has a way to change if warranted in response to inevitable pressures.

Given the context provided in the previous section about the challenges to scaling, where change is piecemeal and innovations unlikely to scale and last, Reading Recovery provides a good case to study implementation in order to better understand the challenges of scaling and sustaining.

Reading Recovery's 30-year implementation in the United States

Today, Reading Recovery is implemented in five countries. Reconstructions have been developed for both the Spanish and French languages. In Spanish, it is called *Descubriendo la Lectura* and in French, it is *Intervention Préventive en Lecture-écriture* (D'Agostino & Rodgers, 2014a). Table 1 displays the implementation of Reading Recovery in the United States as of 2014–2015.

Initial implementation

Reading Recovery's first implementation in the United States began with a problem. Professors at Ohio State seeking an alternative to retention and traditional remedial reading programs visited New Zealand in 1983 to learn more about Reading Recovery, a new program that one of the faculty learned about through a doctoral student's work. By the next year, 1984–1985, Professor Marie Clay and colleague Barbara Watson were in residence at Ohio State to help faculty undertake a pilot project to determine whether the intervention might have the same positive outcomes. In that pilot year, 14 teachers and seven teacher leaders were trained in six schools in one school district (Pinnell, Short, Lyons, & Young, 1986). Based on the positive outcomes in the pilot year, Reading Recovery's implementation doubled in the next school year to 12 elementary schools (adding six new schools and keeping the original six from the pilot), 20 more teachers were trained and added to the cohort of 12 previously trained teachers, and three new teacher leaders were added. The expansion, however, remained limited to the same school district (Pinnell et al., 1986).

For many educational innovations, this is where the scaling story typically ends. The new intervention grows to a number of schools, typically nested within a local school district and rarely going

Table 1. Total participation in Reading Recovery in the United States, 2014–2015.

Entity	Number
States	42
Universities	19
Regional teacher training sites	243
School districts	1,205
Schools	3,735
Teacher leaders	298
Teachers	5,875
Students	46,849

Source. International Data Evaluation Center (2015).

beyond (see Elmore, 1996). Reading Recovery, on the other hand, expanded from just six schools in one school district in 1984–1985 to 3,735 schools in 1,205 districts located in 42 states by 2014–2015. Over that 30-year history of implementation, Reading Recovery's pattern of expansion has not been one of steady growth but, rather, one that has waxed and waned over time. I describe that pattern in more detail next and then compare Reading Recovery's implementation to definitions of scaling that were described in the previous section.

Exponential expansion: 1985–2000

Based on the positive outcomes of the pilot study in 1985–1986, Reading Recovery was selected by the U.S. Department of Education's National Diffusion Network (NDN) in 1987 as a demonstrator project. Demonstrator projects were selected for funding based on their promising results and with the goal of making them more widely available beyond their local implementations. NDN funding was used to support the training of new faculty at universities outside Ohio, thereby helping to replicate Ohio State's three-tiered professional development model in other states across the country (D'Agostino & Rodgers, 2013). Even after NDN was eventually eliminated by Congress, Reading Recovery continued to expand at an exponential rate so that by 2000, it was implemented in all 50 states in over 10,000 schools (see Table 2).

There was no design plan for scaling; any elementary school was eligible to have a teacher train in Reading Recovery, provided the teacher was within traveling distance of a regional teacher training site. In this 15-year period of steady expansion, the number of teachers trained in Reading Recovery increased from 21 to 18,861 (see Table 3).

Steady decline: 2000–2010

The number of teachers and schools participating in Reading Recovery began to decline in 2000, and for the first time, the intervention was not growing but rather shrinking in size. As can be seen in Table 3, the number of children taught and teachers and teacher leaders trained declined, and there was a related decline in the number of schools, districts, and states implementing the program.

Reading Recovery's decline during this period was most likely related to its exclusion from Reading First funding, a federal funding source that awarded state-level grants to increase achievement of beginning readers by the end of Grade 3. According to a report released in 2006 following a federal investigation by the Office of the Inspector General (OIG) into the management of Reading First funding, the composition of the expert review panels that were established to award Reading First funding not only heavily favored a particular approach to reading instruction, but also specifically excluded other approaches, including Reading Recovery. According to the Inspector General's Report (OIG, 2006):

> A few days before the Department publicly announced the panelists it had chosen to serve, one of the Department-nominated panelists contacted the Reading First Director and shared his strong bias against Reading Recovery and his strategy for responding to any State that planned to include Reading Recovery in its application. The Reading First Director responded: "I really like the way you're viewing/approaching this, and not just because it matches my own approach :-), I swear!" This individual later served as the panel chair for the subpanel that reviewed Wisconsin's State application and in response to the State's plans to use Reading Recovery, he included an 11-page negative review of Reading Recovery in his official comments on the application. (p. 18)

Table 2. Reading Recovery implementation by 5-year intervals: Schools, districts, and states.

	Districts		Schools		States	
	n	% Change	n	% Change	n	% Change
84–85	1		6		1	
89–90	332	33,000	892	15,000	18	1,700
94–95	2,543	665	7,784	773	44	144
99–00	3,268	29	10,664	37	50	14
04–05	2,614	−25	8,139	−24	50	0
09–10	1,721	−34	5,412	−34	44	−12

Table 3. Reading Recovery implementation: Students*, teachers, teacher leaders.

	Students*		Teachers		Teacher Leaders	
	n	% Change	n	% Change	N	% Change
84–85 (Pilot)	56		21		7	–
89–90	7,778	6,970	1,163	7,169	54	
94–95	81,220	944	12,084	939	510	844.4
99–00	146,927	80	18,861	56	728	42.8
04–05	115,717	−21	13,823	−26	600	−17.6
09–10	73,248	−37	8,785	−36	411	−31.5

*Excludes non-Reading Recovery students taught during the rest of the instructional day.

Reading First was funded by Congress from 2002 to 2007 for nearly $1 billion, and during that time period Reading Recovery, along with other programs that were deemed to be not scientifically research-based, was excluded from state proposals for Reading First funding (see Cummins, 2007; May et al., 2013; OIG, 2006).

These preferred programs had a systematic phonics approach, and despite the fact that Reading First legislation did not identify systematic phonics approaches as being scientifically based in reading research, funding was directed to particular programs that focused on that approach. The OIG (2006) highlighted this inappropriate favoritism for particular programs to be funded and others to be excluded:

> The Assistant Secretary for OESE planned for the Reading First Guidance to include language that was not in the statute and exclude language that was in the statute. After reviewing a revision to the Department's draft of the Reading First Guidance, the Assistant Secretary for OESE wrote to the Reading First Director, "under reading first plan. i'd (sic) like not to say 'this must include early intervention and reading remediation materials' which I (sic) think could be read as 'reading recovery' [a reading program]. even (sic) if it says this in the law, i'd (sic) like it taken out." (p. 15)

It seems reasonable to conclude that Reading Recovery's steady decline in this time period was related to its exclusion from federal funding; after all, the program's effectiveness had not diminished, nor had the design changed. Between 2002 and 2004, the number of students served by Reading Recovery decreased by nearly 25,000 from 149,038 students to 124,730 (Gómez-Bellengé, Rodgers, & Schulz, 2004) as school districts began to drop Reading Recovery in favor of adopting programs that were favored for federal Reading First funding. Even under this pressure, however, Reading Recovery did not disappear.

Targeted expansion: 2010–2015

Reading Recovery's second infusion of funding for expansion (NDN being the first) came in 2010 with the U.S. Department of Education's Office of Innovation's $45.6 million, 5-year scale-up award to investigators at The Ohio State University (see Rodgers & D'Agostino, 2011). A required $10.3 million match was also raised from the private sector to achieve the grant goals. The award was given to scale projects that had strong evidence of effectiveness. The expansion during this period was different from any other time in Reading Recovery's history, in that, this time, particular schools—the lowest performing in the country—were targeted for implementation. Specifically, the funding was intended to train 3,690 more teachers in Reading Recovery in high priority schools across the country, including very low achieving Title I schools, schools in rural districts, and schools with high populations of English Language Learners.

Along with the training activities, the funding supported an external evaluation of Reading Recovery, the first large evaluation of Reading Recovery since the 1994 study conducted by Pinnell, Lyons, DeFord, Bryk, and Seltzer, and, arguably, the largest educational evaluation that has ever been conducted (see May et al., 2015). This external evaluation was conducted by investigators at the Consortium for Policy Research in Education (CPRE). The study's design employed a multisite randomized

Table 4. Teachers trained, students taught with Investing in Innovation's grant.

Year	Teachers	1–1 Students	Other Students
1	300	2,400	12,600
2	905	8,480	44,520
3	876	12,832	67,368
4	805	17,352	91,098
5	861	23,000	120,000
Total	3,747	62,064	335,586

controlled trial to evaluate student progress in the intervention and a regression discontinuity design to follow students after the intervention. CPRE is also conducting an evaluation of the fidelity of Reading Recovery's implementation, its impact on teacher beliefs, and the spread of knowledge beyond the intervention's setting into the other part of the teacher's instructional day (see May et al., 2013; May et al., 2014; May et al., 2015). This is the first time that depth of change and spread of ideas, features of scaling espoused by Coburn (2003), will be measured in any innovation.

The grant goal of training 3,690 teachers was surpassed by the end of the grant period, as can be seen in Table 4.

The teachers who were trained worked in a variety of schools, with most of the schools fitting one or more of the grant's highest priority categories to target persistently low performing schools (see Table 5).

By the end of the grant period, of the 3,747 teachers who were trained, 2,833 remained in the Reading Recovery role, for an overall attrition rate of 22.7% (see Table 6).

I discuss this attrition rate in greater depth later in this article, when I outline the lessons learned about scaling from Reading Recovery's case and discuss the place of attrition in scaling.

Features of Reading Recovery's implementation pattern

At the outset of this article, I outlined several features of scaling articulated by those working in the field of educational reform, and I noted that, taken together, these definitions of scaling, and what it means to be at scale, present a challenge to developers of new educational initiatives. What does it mean to create deep change and spread ideas throughout a system, beyond the innovation? Is it possible to scale up in more varied settings and maintain the quality of effectiveness that made it possible to expand in the first place? In this next section, I consider the case of Reading Recovery's scaling in light of those challenging ideas, and, afterwards, I offer a fresh synthesis of what it means to scale.

Effectiveness maintained and demonstrated over time

As discussed earlier, Schneider and McDonald's (2007) definition of scaling goes beyond uptake in more varied settings. In addition, they note that as the innovation is scaled to different kinds of schools with different kinds of students, it ought to maintain its effectiveness over time.

Over the last 30 years, four evaluations of Reading Recovery have been conducted that meet the US Department of Education's What Works Clearinghouse's (WWC, 2013) highest level of evidence

Table 5. School participation by i3 grant priority*.

Priority	Schools
School Improvement Grant eligible	106 (4%)
Title I	215 (9%)
Rural	374 (16%)
Sizable population of English as a second language	836 (35%)
Title I Program improvement (Year 1 or 2)	369 (16%)
Other schools	888 (38%)
Total	2,360

*Schools may fall into more than one category.

Table 6. i3 teacher attrition*.

	n (%)
Teachers trained 2010–2015	3,747
Teachers still in role as of June 2015	2,833 (77.3%)
Teachers exited	830 (22.7%)
Reasons for exiting:	
Involuntary (School or district decision)	433 (11.6%)
Voluntary (Personal teacher decision)	392 (10.5%)
Other (Not specified)	5 (< 0.1%)

*As of June, 2015 before audit of final year.

standards. These evaluations, conducted over time and in various locales across the country, all document Reading Recovery's positive effects on the students served (see Table 7).

The WWC's reviews show that Reading Recovery produces the largest impact on student reading skills of any intervention reviewed (WWC, 2013), making it one of the most promising reading interventions available for children. And, because the four studies have been conducted at about 10-year intervals starting with the initial implementation and ending with the current year, it is reasonable to conclude that the innovation has maintained its effectiveness as it has scaled over time, across locales, and with a more varied student population. (See D'Agostino & Harmey's [2016] article, this issue, for a quantitative synthesis of the rigorous studies that have been conducted worldwide.)

Uptake in more varied school settings

As described in the previous section, another feature of Schneider and McDonald's (2007) definition of scaling is that, over time, the innovation is implemented in more varied settings than its original setting. Twelve elementary schools were involved in the first year of Reading Recovery's implementation, 1985–1986 (one year after the pilot year). All 12 schools were in an urban setting, and each school had more than a 50% non-White enrollment (Pinnell et al., 1986).

As Table 8 displays, however, Reading Recovery is now implemented almost evenly across a variety of schools in rural, suburban, and urban areas. Variation in student demographics was also evenly

Table 7. Reading Recovery effectiveness over time: What Works Clearinghouse's accepted studies.

Study	Design	Sample Size	Location	Measures	Alphabetics	Fluency	Comp	General Reading
Pinnell, DeFord, and Lyons, 1988	RCT	187 students 12 schools	1 state	OSELA – all subtests CTBS Vocab CTBS Comp	−.24–.41		.56–.57	.56–.92
Pinnell, Lyons, DeFord, Bryk, and Seltzer, 1994	RCT	403 students 43 schools	1 state	OSELA - Dictation Woodcock Gates-MacGinitie Reading Test	.89			.49–.65
Schwartz, 2005	RCT	94 students	14 states	OSELA Phoneme Segmentation Phoneme Deletion SORT – R Degrees of Reading Power	.41–1.37	.93–2.49	.14	.95–1.16
May et al., 2015	RCT	866 students 147 schools	44 states	ITBS Words ITBS Comp ITBS Total Reading Score			.55	.55–.61

Note. OSELA = *An Observation Survey of Early Literacy Achievement* (Clay, 2013); CTBS = Comprehensive Tests of Basic Skills; SORT = Slosson Oral Reading Test; ITBS = Illinois Test of Basic Skills.

Table 8. Description of schools and students: 1985–1986 and 2014–2015.

Description	1985–1986		2014–2015	
	n	Col %	n	Col %
School locale:				
No data			273	
Urban city	12	100%	985	28.5%
Suburban/Large town	0	0%	1,140	32.9%
Small town/Rural	0	0%	1,335	38.6%
School minority enrollment:				
No data			291	
0–5.0	0	0%	384	11.2%
5.0–20.0	0	0%	988	28.7%
20.0–50.0	10	83.3%	997	29%
50.0–100.0	2	16.7%	1,073	31.2%

Note. Differences between total group *n* and variable totals represent missing data for that variable.

distributed across schools by 2014–2015 (International Data Evaluation Center, 2015). About one-third of schools with Reading Recovery had between 5% and 20% minority enrollment, another third between 20% and 50%, and another third had between half and 100% minority enrollment.

English language learner status data were not collected in 1985–1986, so it is not possible to examine change over time in terms of that demographic feature. We do know, however, that in 2014–2015, about 17% of all students who received Reading Recovery lessons were from homes where a language other than English was spoken, and that this figure is nearly double the current national percentage of all public school students participating in programs for English language learners (National Center for Education Statistics [NCES], 2015; see Table 9). It seems likely, therefore, that over time, the population of Reading Recovery students has become more varied over time in terms of language status from the original cohort in 1985.

Not only has Reading Recovery scaled in terms of the numbers of schools that implement it, from 12 schools in the first year to 3,735 in the current year, but the schools that implement it are much more varied from the original setting both in terms of locale and student population (defined as proportion of minority student population and English learner status).

Spread of ideas and norms for practice

It is difficult, perhaps impossible, to prove that Reading Recovery's ideas and norms have spread beyond its setting to influence general practices in education. A strong case can be made, however, that at least three current trends have been influenced by Reading Recovery.

One example of Reading Recovery's influence may be found in the response-to-intervention approach (RTI), an alternative method to identifying children with learning disabilities as described by Fuchs and Fuchs (2006). Rather than relying on scores on intelligence measures to identify children as learning disabled, the RTI approach relies on children's responsiveness to intervention to make referral decisions; children who do not respond well to the more intensive instruction provided by Reading Recovery (more intensive than classroom instruction) can then be more reliably referred on for additional assessment and possible placement in special-education settings.

Table 9. Language spoken at home, 2012–2013.

Description	Reading Recovery Students	
Language	n	Col %
English	38,567	83%
Spanish	5,821	12%
Some other language	2,256	5%

Source. D'Agostino and Harmey (2015).

In fact, Vellutino (2010) noted that Reading Recovery is one of the first examples of an RTI approach to identifying and teaching children with reading difficulties. He wrote:

> Marie Clay's Reading Recovery, as a vehicle for identifying children at risk for long-term reading difficulties and thus in need of special educational services, predated these intervention studies. ... It must be acknowledged that Marie Clay was actually the first reading researcher to use RTI to identify children who might be afflicted by organically based reading difficulties, although Reading Recovery, as originally conceived, was not designed for this purpose. Thus, her contribution to the RTI movement was seminal and certainly set the stage for subsequent intervention research that served to give this movement even greater momentum. (p. 7)

Reading Recovery's ideas and practices have also been innovated and spread to other layers of instruction, including classroom and small-group settings. Literacy Collaborative, a well known professional development program to create expert teachers in classroom settings, is informed by Reading Recovery's instructional practices and was developed by some of the early implementers of Reading Recovery in the United States (Biancarosa, Bryk, & Dexter, 2010; Hough et al., 2013). In addition, Leveled Literacy Intervention (LLI) is based on Reading Recovery's approach, but it is designed for children whose reading difficulties are not as severe as those of children in Reading Recovery and who thus can respond to instruction in small group settings (Ransford-Kaldon, Flynt, & Ross, 2011). LLI is also designed for children in elementary grades, not only first grade. In short, it can be argued that Reading Recovery's design has spread to other instructional settings and grades due to the innovative work of the original implementers of Reading Recovery in the United States.

Another example of the spread of Reading Recovery's practices can be found in the uptake of Clay's oral reading assessment tool called *running records* (Clay, 2000). Clay developed this tool very early on in her research, and it later became a part of daily Reading Recovery lessons so that teachers could daily monitor student progress, analyze their reading development, and plan instruction. The use of this tool, which requires the teacher to systematically observe and record every reading behavior and analyze what children are doing as they read, is now so widespread that often, when running records are mentioned in published scholarly papers, no one is credited for them; the developer is now often forgotten. In response, the 2000 publication *Running Records* (Clay, 2000) includes this note under the copyright: "Marie Clay asserts the moral right to be known as the author of Running Records and this material."

Creating deep change

A final feature of Reading Recovery's implementation that relates to the definitions of scaling presented at the outset of this article has to do with creating deep change in practices. As Coburn (2003) asserted, to say a program has scaled, one should expect the innovation to have brought about deep change in practice, going beyond such surface changes as having more time in a reading block or changing the reading program used in a classroom. A program at scale ought to be effecting deep change in teacher beliefs.

As I wrote earlier in this article, in addition to evaluating the impact of Reading Recovery on student reading achievement, CPRE, the external evaluators for the i3 grant to scale up Reading Recovery, are also conducting a qualitative evaluation of the quality of the program's implementation (May et al., 2013). This dimension of the evaluation, which includes the collection of activity logs, interviews, and survey data from teachers training in Reading Recovery, helps to get at perceptions about the depth of change by individual teachers as a result of implementing Reading Recovery.

May et al. (2013) described two themes that emerged at the individual level, both of which suggest a deep impact on beliefs and practices. Teachers reported adopting a new perspective on literacy, in some cases a fresh perspective on teaching reading skills. May et al. quoted one teacher who said that participating in Reading Recovery "led her to re-conceptualize the way children learn to read" (p. 97). Another theme that emerged from their analysis of change at the individual level had to do with learning translatable skills, another example of deep change (and perhaps also a good example of change spreading). May et al. wrote:

> Nearly 72 percent of all RR teachers who responded to the survey reported that implementing RR improved their general literacy instruction to a great extent (i.e., the top category on a four-point Likert scale), and many reported feeling reassured about their skills as reading teachers overall. RR teachers who were interviewed noted that the use of RR strategies and language particularly enhanced their literacy instruction in small group settings. (p. 98)

Although Coburn (2003) was referring to deep change in teacher beliefs as a feature of scaling, there is also growing evidence that Reading Recovery instruction also brings about deep change in students' agency as readers and their motivation to read. (See Bates, D'Agostino, Gambrell, & Xu, 2016.)

Summary of Reading Recovery's scaling pattern

Reading Recovery's implementation over 30 years has not been one of steady growth and expansion; instead, it can be characterized as waxing and waning over the years. Its scaling pattern, however, contains many of the features described earlier in this article as necessary for innovations to scale and does not follow the typical pattern of failing after a short period of implementation in a local setting.

Why innovations scale: A fresh synthesis from Reading Recovery's case

It is clear from the literature reviewed earlier in this article that scaling up an educational innovation is challenging work. Reading Recovery's implementation history is unique in that it is still in wide use in U.S. schools after 30 years of continuous implementation, despite aggressive efforts to limit its implementation during the Reading First years. Yet a major impetus for the Office of Innovation's Investing in Innovation grant structure is to develop, validate, and scale proven programs. What lessons might be taken away from Reading Recovery's case that might inform other educational innovations as they attempt to scale up?

An innovation cannot scale without a design

An innovation needs a well articulated design; otherwise, it is not possible for the innovation to be replicated with fidelity, nor to change in response to new evidence about what works (Stringfield & Datnow, 1998; Wilson & Daviss, 1994). Not only does the innovation need a well articulated design, but, in addition, the design has to allow for change to occur, as Stringfield and Datnow (1998) noted. Having a design and a process for change will help guard against the constant pressure to pare down essential features of a design or substitute inferior ingredients simply for the sake of change. (See Cohen, Peurach, Glazer, Gates, & Goldin, 2013, for more on the role of design in the success of educational innovations to scale and sustain.)

Examine, maintain, and demonstrate effectiveness while scaling

A hallmark of Reading Recovery's implementation over 30 years is that it has maintained its impact on students' literacy achievement. Why might this demonstrated impact be important to scaling? As Guskey (1986) noted, effectiveness changes teachers' beliefs, and new beliefs are needed to change teachers' instructional practices. This need for demonstrated effectiveness means that data ought to be collected and analyzed from a program's inception and continually thereafter. Reading Recovery implementers in the United States began collecting data from the first year, and data have been collected and outcomes reported every year since then on every child served in Reading Recovery, regardless of outcome in the program (see https://www.idecweb.us/Publications.aspx for evaluation publications).

Why continue to examine effectiveness once a program's positive impact has been demonstrated? It is possible that the program's impact will lessen over time. For example, Lemons, Fuchs, Gilbert, and Fuchs (2014) conducted a retrospective analysis of five randomized control treatment design studies, conducted over a 9-year period, of the program Kindergarten Peer-Assisted Learning Strategies. Lemons and colleagues were surprised to find what they described as a "disappearing difference" (p. 6) between the treatment and control students. They hypothesized that the program began to perform less well after it was implemented for several years because, over time, the counterfactual changed. In other words, the control students were improving over time, perhaps because the program's positive effects were beginning to spread to other instructional settings in the schools.

A disappearing difference is becoming apparent in Reading Recovery's data, as well. D'Agostino and Rodgers (2014b), using first-grade multiple cohort data from the same 2,358 schools implementing Reading Recovery over a 10-year period, found that the achievement gap between the lowest achieving students selected for Reading Recovery and comparison cohorts has steadily decreased on literacy measures emphasizing item knowledge. D'Agostino and Rodgers hypothesized that kindergarten instruction may have changed over the years to place more of an emphasis on item knowledge (letter identification, letter-sound relationships), a reasonable hunch given the emphasis of Reading First on beginning reading instruction during the same time period. At the same time, D'Agostino and Rodgers note a widening gap on measures of text level reading between low and average achieving students at the beginning of first grade.

A changing counterfactual means that the needs of the population that existed at the program's inception have changed, and this difference should be accounted for in terms of the innovation's instructional emphases if the program will continue to be effective and relevant.

Expect attrition

Clearly, individuals will change jobs, and attrition should be expected. How much attrition, however, might one reasonably expect when scaling an innovation? The best metric available is the NCES's Teacher Follow-Up Survey (NCES, 2015), a nationally representative sample survey of public and private K–12 teachers who, in the previous year, participated in NCES's Schools and Staffing Survey (NCES, 2015). The Follow-Up Survey reports the number and percentage of teachers who were in the role in the previous year, or stayed in the same teaching role the following year, or moved to another teaching position, or left the profession altogether.

In 2013, the most recent year that NCES data are available, 8.7% of primary school teachers moved to another position from the one they had in the previous school year, and an additional 7.4% left the teaching position altogether, for a combined attrition rate of about 16.1% of primary school teachers who were no longer in the same teaching position that they had in the previous school year. By comparison, 22.7% of teachers trained in Reading Recovery with the grant were no longer in the role by the end of the grant period, making the grant attrition about 6% higher than what one might expect in the general teaching population.

I followed up with teacher leaders to learn more about the underlying reasons for attrition from Reading Recovery during the i3 grant period from 2010 to 2015. Recall from Table 6 that there were two main reasons for teachers leaving the Reading Recovery role after training with i3 funds: 10.5% left for a personal reason and 11.6% left involuntarily because of a school or district decision. When one considers only the attrition rate for personal reasons for leaving the Reading Recovery role (10.5%), then attrition is lower than the national rate of attrition from teaching (16.1%). That proportion, 10.5%, however, accounts only for about half of the attrition from Reading Recovery during the grant; the rest, 11.6%, left involuntarily, because of a district- or school-level decision.

I surveyed teacher leaders to find out more about the reasons for the 11.6% who left involuntarily; the survey results are displayed in Table 10.

Table 10. Reasons underlying involuntary decisions to leave Reading Recovery role.

	N	% of Involuntary Attrition	% of Total Attrition
Total attrition	830		
Total involuntary attrition	433		
Survey responses	159		
Program design did not fit school environment (New administration with different philosophy, wanted expertise to be shared with more children, did not want to teach daily lessons)	114	19.1	13.7
Personnel reason (Moved the teacher to another position due to: redundancy, promotion, teacher not meeting new state requirements)	41		
	9.4%	4.9	
Program had poor results	3	< 0%	< 0%
Funding lost	1	< 0%	< 0%

It is important to note that the response rate to the survey accounted for only about one third of the involuntary attrition. Yet, a clear trend seems to emerge. "Program had poor results" was rarely a stated reason for a district decision to drop the program. Rather, administrators more frequently cited an issue with some feature of the program's design not fitting with a new administration's school environment as the reason for dropping.

The reason most often cited, that the administrator wanted the teacher to work with more students, and that it was considered too costly to work with students one-to-one, seems disingenuous when one considers that the Reading Recovery role is for about 2.5 hrs a day only, and that during the other half of the day the teachers work with small groups or classrooms. In fact, according to the most recent national evaluation of Reading Recovery, teachers working in Reading Recovery typically taught another 40 students during the year, in addition to the 8–10 students taught in Reading Recovery, for a total on average of 48 students in a year (D'Agostino & Harmey, 2015). This is a far greater number of students than the number served by a typical classroom teacher in one year.

Instead, it seems far more likely, particularly given the challenges to scaling reviewed at the outset of this article, that many of the new school or district administrators wanted to bring in their own initiative, regardless of evidence. Even with demonstrated and accepted effectiveness, and with a financial investment in the teacher's professional development, it seems that proven innovations are not immune to passing fads because, as Cohen and Ball (2007) suggested, the educational environment is complex and fragmented.

A lesson that can be taken from Reading Recovery's case, then, is that, often, the reason for a district dropping an innovation might not be the innovation's effectiveness, but simply the second reason offered by Cohen and Ball (2007): The educational environment for making decisions about what programs to implement is often chaotic (Glazer & Peurach, 2013). It seems reasonable to conclude that, as long as administrators have no fiscal incentive to take up evidence-based practices, an attrition rate over and above the typical rate of teachers leaving the profession, unfortunately, should be expected.

Develop many local heroes

Stringfield and Datnow (1998) warned that innovations that rely on individual heroes to champion the program are likely to fail over time. Reading Recovery's case suggests a variation on that theme: Having many local heroes. Reading Recovery's design contains a more decentralized structure; there really is no headquarters. Rather, the replication of its three-tiered network of professional development from state to state relies on local champions. A school district in Lincoln, Nebraska, or Akron, Ohio, for that matter, is more likely to care about a local leader, rather than a small group of faculty members at Ohio State. In this regard, Reading Recovery has nearly 300 teacher leaders across the country who are extraordinarily talented and who are well prepared to teach other teachers how to use the instructional practices. Rather than one or two individuals, Reading Recovery has a network of talented people, the teacher leaders, who are respected locally and who carry out the intensive, heroic work associated with maintaining the program's fidelity and effectiveness.

According to Clay (1994), the teacher leader is the agent of redirection because of the pivotal role in redirecting learning across the system; every part of the system has to change, including the child learning, the teacher learning, the system learning, and the community learning. Clay (1994) said that teacher leaders are redirecting systems because they "teach children, train teachers, educate the local educators, negotiate the implementation of the program, act as advocates for whatever cannot be compromised in the interests of effective results, and talk to the public and media, correcting misconceptions" (p. 127). The teacher leader, therefore, is responsible for orchestrating fundamental changes in the system, the kind of reform where things that really matter are changed, which, as Fullan (1993) has noted, is so critical for reform to occur.

Summary

It seems clear that, to scale up an innovation, it must have a design that allows the innovation to manage the tension between changing and staying the same, a tension to be expected if the design is a successful one. Having a design is what allows the innovation to expand and contract and expand again. From this perspective, innovations never finally reach scale and never finally become institutionalized in a setting. Instead, scaling is an organic process in which the innovation's implementation can be expected to wax and wane.

Clay (1994), writing 20 years ago, when Reading Recovery's implementation was just 10 years old in the United States, wrote about the importance of understanding scaling and sustaining an educational innovation, in addition to having evidence about results. She wrote:

> In the decade ahead the half-life of the program will be plotted. Many educational programs are not developed, explored, and continued, and the easy summary is that nothing works. … Why do critics consider it important that the innovation take account of all emerging theoretical guesses and the evidence from experiments under special conditions when they give little or no attention to theories about mounting the innovation in a system, replicability, variance in different settings, and how the program can change in response to new evidence and yet be considered the same program? (p. 139)

Two clear lessons about scaling emerge from Reading Recovery's case. One is that evidence is important but not sufficient. Having evidence about effectiveness is necessary, but evidence alone will not sustain nor grow an innovation. Evidence will, however, make it easier for systems to take up the program and somewhat harder for new administrators to abolish it. And, from a moral and ethical standpoint, and because improving education is our shared goal, it is hard to imagine why anyone would want to scale up an innovation without knowing whether it works, and whether it continues to be effective in settings that vary from the original site. The second lesson, then, is when designing an innovation for schools, the developer's attention should go beyond the impact on student achievement to thinking about how to scale. Reading Recovery's case demonstrates that scaling and sustaining are possible, but that the process should be viewed as an organic one and not a state that can be finally achieved.

Acknowledgments

This article was prepared with the support of a U.S. Department of Education i3 award to Jerome D'Agostino, Principal Investigator, to scale up Reading Recovery, Office of Innovation and Improvement (Grant/Award Number #U396A100027).

References

Bates, C. C., D'Agostino, J. V., Gambrell, L., & Xu, M. (2016). Reading Recovery: Exploring the effects on first-graders' reading motivation and achievement. *Journal of Education for Students Placed At Risk, 21*, 47–59.
Biancarosa, G., Bryk, A. S., & Dexter, E. R. (2010). Assessing the value-added effects of literacy collaborative professional development on student learning. *Elementary School Journal, 111*, 7–34. doi: 10.1086/653468
Brown, K. J., Morris, D., & Fields, M. (2005). Intervention after grade 1: Serving increased numbers of struggling readers effectively. *Journal of Literacy Research, 37*, 61–94. doi: 10.1207/s15548430jlr3701_3
Clay, M. M. (1994). The wider implications of an educational innovation. *Literacy Teaching and Learning, 1*, 121–141.
Clay, M. M. (2000). *Running records for classroom teachers*. Portsmouth, NH: Heinemann.
Clay, M. M. (2013). *An observation survey of early literacy achievement* (3rd ed.). Portsmouth, NH: Heinemann.
Coburn, C. E. (2003). Rethinking scale: Moving beyond numbers to deep and lasting change. *Educational Researcher, 32* (6), 3–12. doi:10.3102/0013189×032006003
Cohen, C., & Ball, D. (2007). Educational innovation and the problem of scale. In B. Schneider & S. K. McDonald (Eds.), *Scale-up in education: Ideas in principle* (Vol. 1; pp. 19–36). Lanham, MD: Rowman & Littlefield.
Cohen, D. K., Peurach, D. J., Glazer, J. L., Gates, K. E., & Goldin, S. (2013). *Improvement by design: The promise of better schools*. Chicago, IL: University of Chicago Press.
Cummins, J. (2007). Pedagogies for the poor? Realigning reading instruction for low-income students with scientifically based reading research. *Educational Researcher, 36*, 564–572. doi: 10.3102/0013189×07313156
D'Agostino, J. V. (2012). Technical review committee confirms highest NCRTI ratings for Observation Survey of Early Literacy Achievement. *Journal of Reading Recovery, 1* (2), 53–56.
D'Agostino, J. V., & Harmey, S. (2015). *Reading Recovery and Descubriendo la Lectura National Report 2013–2014* (IDEC Rep. No. 2015–01). Columbus, OH: The Ohio State University, International Data Evaluation Center.
D'Agostino, J. V., & Harmey, S. J. (2016). An international meta-analysis of Reading Recovery. *Journal of Education for Students Placed At Risk, 21*, 29–46.

D'Agostino, J. V., & Murphy, J. A. (2004). A meta-analysis of Reading Recovery in United States schools. *Educational Evaluation and Policy Analysis, 26*, 23–38. doi: 10.3102/01623737026001023

D'Agostino, J. V., & Rodgers, E. (2013, July). *Scaling-up Reading Recovery*. Paper presented at the meeting of the International Reading Recovery Institute, Sydney, Australia.

D'Agostino, J. V., & Rodgers, E. (2014a, June). *Integrating English learners in Reading Recovery*. Paper presented at the annual meeting of the i3 Project Director's Meeting, Washington, DC.

D'Agostino, J. V., & Rodgers, E. (2014b, April). *Using multiple-cohort data to construct a nationally representative literacy profile of early readers*. Paper presented at the meeting of the American Educational Research Association, Philadelphia, PA.

D'Agostino, J. V., & Rodgers, E. (2015, June). *Affordances and challenges of providing high quality professional development to teachers in rural areas*. Paper presented at the annual meeting of the i3 Project Director's Meeting, Washington, DC.

Datnow, A., & Stringfield, S. (2000). Working together for reliable school reform. *Journal of Education for Students Placed At Risk, 5*, 183–204. doi:10.1080/10824669.2000.9671386

Denton, C. A., Vaughn, S., & Fletcher, J. M. (2003). Bringing research-based practice in reading intervention to scale. *Learning Disabilities: Research & Practice, 18*, 201–211. doi: 10.1111/1540-5826.00075

Elmore, R. F. (1996). Getting to scale with good educational practice. *Harvard Educational Review, 66*(1), 1–26. doi:10.17763/haer.66.1.g73266758j348t33

Fuchs, D., & Fuchs, L. S. (2006). Introduction to Response to Intervention: What, why, and how valid is it? *Reading Research Quarterly, 41*(1), 93–99. doi:10.1598/rrq.41.1.4

Fullan, M. (1993). *Change forces: Probing the depth of educational reform*. New York, NY: Falmer Press.

Gersten, R., Chard, D., & Baker, S. (2000). Factors enhancing sustained use of research-based instructional practices. *Journal of Learning Disabilities, 33*, 445–57. doi: 10.1177/002221940003300505

Glazer, J. L., & Peurach, D. J. (2013). School improvement networks as a strategy for large-scale education reform: The role of educational environments. *Educational Policy, 27*, 676–710. doi:10.1177/0895904811429283

Gómez-Bellengé, F. X., Rodgers, E., & Schulz, M. (2004). *Reading Recovery and Descubriendo la Lectura National Report, 2003–2004*. Columbus, OH: National Data Evaluation Center.

Guskey, T. R. (1986). Staff development and the process of teacher change. *Educational Researcher, 15*(5), 5–12. doi:10.3102/0013189×015005005

Hough, H. J., Kerbow, D., Bryk, A., Pinnell, G. S., Rodgers, E., Dexter, E., … Fountas, I. (2013). Assessing teacher practice and development: The case of comprehensive literacy instruction. *School Effectiveness and School Improvement, 24*, 452–485. doi: 10.1080/09243453.2012.731004

International Data Evaluation Center. (2015). 2014–2015 *National Summary Report for the United States*. Columbus, OH: The Ohio State University. Retrieved from https://www.idecweb.us/publications.aspx

Lemons, C. J., Fuchs, D., Gilbert, J. K., & Fuchs, L. S. (2014). Evidence-based practices in a changing world: Reconsidering the counterfactual in education research. *Educational Researcher, 43*, 242–252. doi: 10.3102/0013189×14539189

May, H., Goldsworthy, H., Armijo, M., Gray, A., Sirinides, P., Blalock, T. J., … Sam, C. (2014). *Evaluation of the i3 scale-up of Reading Recovery* (Research Report No. RR-79). Retrieved from http://www.cpre.org/sites/default/files/researchreport/2036_rryear2report.pdf

May, H., Gray, A., Gillespie, J. N., Sirinides, P., Sam, C., Goldsworthy, H., … Tognatta, N. (2013). *Evaluation of the i3 scale-up of Reading Recovery Year One Report, 2011–12*. Philadelphia, PA: Consortium for Policy Research in Education.

May, H., Gray, A., Sirinides, P., Goldsworthy, H., Armijo, M., Sam, C., … Tognatta, N. (2015). Year one results from the multisite randomized evaluation of the i3 scale-up of Reading Recovery. *American Educational Research Journal, 52*, 547–581. doi: 10.3102/0002831214565788

National Center for Education Statistics. (2015, March). *Local education agency universe survey, 2002–03 through 2012–13* [Data tables]. Retrieved from http://nces.ed.gov/programs/digest/d14/tables/dt14_204.20.asp

National Center on Response to Intervention. (2014). *Screening charts*. Retrieved from http://www.rti4success.org/resources/tools-charts/screening-tools-chart

Office of the Inspector General. (2006). *The Reading First program's grant application process. Final inspection report* (Report No. EDOIG/ I13-F0017). Washington, DC: US Department of Education.

Petroski, H. (2001). Success and failure in engineering. *National Forum, Winter*, 10–17.

Petroski, H. (2006). *Success through failure: The paradox of design*. Princeton, NJ: Princeton University Press.

Pinnell, G. S., DeFord, D. E., & Lyons, C. A. (1988). *Reading Recovery: Early intervention for at-risk first graders* (Educational Research Service monograph). Arlington, VA: Educational Research Service.

Pinnell, G. S., Lyons, C. A., DeFord, D. E., Bryk, A. S., & Seltzer, M. (1994). Comparing instructional models for the literacy education of high-risk first graders. *Reading Research Quarterly, 29*, 8–39. doi: 10.2307/747736

Pinnell, G. S., Short, K., Lyons, C. A., & Young, P. (1986). *The Reading Recovery project in Columbus Ohio, year 1*. Columbus, OH: The Ohio State University.

Ransford-Kaldon, C., Flynt, E. S., & Ross, C. (2011, March). *A randomized controlled trial of a response-to-intervention (RTI) tier 2 literacy program: Leveled Literacy Intervention (LLI)*. Paper presented at the annual meeting of the Society for Research on Educational Effectiveness, Washington, DC.

Reading Recovery Council of North America. (2014). *Standards and guidelines of Reading Recovery in the United States, 2012.* Retrieved from http://readingrecovery.org/reading-recovery/implementation/standards-a-guidelines

Rodgers, E. (2002). Lessons from a successful reform initiative. In E. Rodgers & G. Pinnell (Eds.), *Learning from teaching in literacy education: New perspectives on professional development* (pp. 158–172). Portsmouth, NH: Heinemann.

Rodgers, E. (2012, November). The role of design in scaling up an educational innovation. In J. V. D'Agostino (Chair), *Scaling up an educational innovation: Analyzing the case of Reading Recovery.* Symposium conducted at the meeting of the Literacy Research Association, San Diego, CA.

Rodgers, E., & D'Agostino, J. (2011). Scaling up Reading Recovery: Poised to start year 2. *Journal of Reading Recovery, 11*(1), 39–42.

Schneider, B., & McDonald, S.-K. (2007). Scale-up in practice: An introduction. In B. Schneider & S. K. McDonald (Eds.), *Scale-up in education: Ideas in principle* (Vol. 1; pp. 1–14). Lanham, MD: Rowman & Littlefield.

Schwartz, R. M. (2005). Literacy learning of at-risk first-grade students in the Reading Recovery early intervention. *Journal of Educational Psychology, 97,* 257–267. doi: 10.1037/0022-0663.97.2.257

Slavin, R., & Madden, N. (2007). Scaling up Success for All: The first sixteen years. In B. Schneider & S. K. McDonald (Eds.), *Scale-up in education: Ideas in practice* (Vol. II; pp. 201–228). Lanham, MD: Rowman & Littlefield.

Stringfield, S., & Datnow, A. (1998). Scaling up school restructuring designs in urban schools. *Education and Urban Society, 30,* 269–76. doi:10.1177/0013124598030003001

U.S. Department of Education, Institute of Education Sciences, What Works Clearinghouse. (2013, July). *Beginning Reading intervention report: Reading Recovery®.* Retrieved from http://whatworks.ed.gov

Vellutino, F. R. (2010). "Learning to be learning disabled": Marie Clay's seminal contribution to the response to intervention approach to identifying specific reading disability. *Journal of Reading Recovery, 10*(1), 5–23.

Wilson, K. G., & Daviss, B. (1994). *Redesigning education.* New York, NY: H. Holt.

An International Meta-Analysis of Reading Recovery

Jerome V. D'Agostino and Sinéad J. Harmey

ABSTRACT
Reading Recovery is one of the most researched literacy programs worldwide. Although there have been at least 4 quantitative reviews of its effectiveness, none have considered all rigorous group-comparison studies from all implementing nations from the late 1970s to 2015. Using a hierarchical linear modeling (HLM) v-known analysis, we examined if effects differed in the United States versus other nations, if experiments yielded larger effects than quasi-experiments, if the effects changed over time, and if the type of outcome mediated the impact estimates. We also considered the sustained effects of the intervention. After reviewing 203 primary studies, we identified 16 that met our criteria, such as treatment fidelity and experimental or high-quality quasi-experimental design. Based on a random effects model, the estimated overall effect was .59, with larger effects for outcomes based on the *Observation Survey* (Clay, 2013), and stronger effects in certain literacy domains, such as text reading, print knowledge, and general literacy. Although United States studies produced a larger point estimate (.61) compared to other countries (.52), and experiments (.69) yielded a larger estimate than quasi-experiments (.43), neither difference was statistically significant. Overall, effects did not change over time, but effects based on the Observation Survey did improve significantly from earlier to later studies. We also found that the long-term effect may diminish, but there were too few studies to estimate the sustained impact with confidence. The .59 overall effect places Reading Recovery in the top 10% in terms of impact of early literacy programs reviewed by the What Works Clearinghouse.

Children who experience difficulties in literacy learning early in their school career are at risk of negative academic and social consequences in later life (Every Child a Chance Trust, 2009; Juel, 1988; Reynolds, Wheldall, & Madelaine, 2010; Stanovich, 1986). Vellutino and Scanlon (2003) stated that research has clearly demonstrated that many reading difficulties of young students are caused by experiential and instructional factors, rather than neurodevelopmental issues. Long-term reading difficulties can be prevented for the large majority of children at risk of later reading difficulties if they are identified early in their school schooling (Vellutino, 2010, p. 17) and provided an effective intervention designed to help them develop effective learning strategies (Scull & Lo Bianco, 2008) that will increase their chances for succeeding in all school subjects.

Reading Recovery (RR) is one such early literacy intervention for children experiencing the most difficulty in literacy learning. It has been implemented in schools in the United States for the past 30 years and originated in New Zealand over 40 years ago. The intervention, based on the research of

Marie Clay, is delivered in the form of one-to-one tutoring by a trained RR teacher. It has been implemented, monitored, and researched in many English-speaking countries, including New Zealand, Australia, the United Kingdom, Ireland, Canada, and the United States (Clay, 2001, p. 217).

RR is one of the most researched early literacy interventions. Besides the numerous primary studies of, commentaries on, and narrative reviews of the intervention, there have been at least four quantitative syntheses conducted to ascertain the impact of RR on student literacy achievement (D'Agostino & Murphy, 2004; Elbaum, Vaughn, Hughes, & Moody, 2000; Slavin, Lake, Davis, & Madden, 2011; What Works Clearinghouse [WWC], 2013). The four prior quantitative analyses have yielded overall effect sizes of .39, .40, .66, and .70 ($M = .54$). Likely, there are many reasons for the variation in effects across the studies, but the most likely reason is that each review did not include the same set of primary studies. Each review was based on different primary-study selection criteria; most, but not all, reviews only included studies conducted in the United States, and only some reviews were limited to group comparison designs. Another contributing factor to the variation is that some reviews excluded studies that yielded effects on Clay's (2013) *Observation Survey of Early Literacy Achievement* (OSELA), which is the assessment system used in RR to identify eligible students and evaluate the overall effect of the intervention. Reviews also varied in the methodological rigor required from primary studies for selection purposes.

To date, no meta-analyses conducted on RR have maintained high methodological rigor selection standards (i.e., included results from experiments or quasi-experiments in which baseline group equivalence was documented or that adjusted posttest means based on pretest differences), that included OSELA and external outcome results, and that considered studies from all countries where RR has been implemented. Furthermore, the results from the largest experimental evaluation of RR to date, which was conducted over the last 4 years, were unavailable to prior reviewers who conducted their research before the primary studies were concluded. The purpose of undertaking a fifth quantitative synthesis was to examine the overall impact on RR in consideration of the limitations of the earlier reviews.

What is RR?

It is a common misconception that the goal of RR is to bring every struggling reader to average reading levels. Instead, according to Clay (2001), RR was designed to "identify a few children for continuing specialist help following one year of good classroom instruction and about twenty weeks of individually designed diagnostic teaching [i.e., RR]" (p. 218). Within this goal, there are two expected outcomes: Either the child responds favorably to the 20 weeks of diagnostic teaching and catches up to peers, or the child does not respond well to RR instruction, and then can more reliably be referred on for further assessment and possible placement in special education (about 28% of participants who complete the 20-week intervention are referred; see D'Agostino & Harmey, 2014). As a result, RR instruction serves as an alternative to IQ testing for the purpose of identifying children with serious reading disabilities, and thus, of reducing the incidence of false positive identification for special educational services.

Given this fundamental goal, one might assume that most evaluation driven by objectives would focus on hypothesized outcomes such as reduced proportions of incorrect special education identification, reduced rates of first-grade retention, and decreased referrals to special education within a few years of implementing the intervention. Instead, most primary studies of RR have been designed to test the hypothesis that all participating children will recover from early achievement struggles by responding positively to the intervention. Also, some studies have attempted to ascertain the sustained effect of RR following the assumption that once the child's growth trajectory is recovered, it should remain within an average band throughout the child's formal schooling.

RR has a strong diagnostic screening system to identify children for the intervention. Following 1 year of schooling, lower performing students are tested with the OSELA, which contains six tasks, including letter identification, hearing and recording sounds in words, writing vocabulary, a word test, concepts about print, and text reading level. There are subtle variations in terms of the assessment according to the country in which the assessment is conducted. For example, in different contexts a different word test is used, standardized to respective national norms. In the United States, a set of standard texts are used to calculate a child's text reading level. In the United Kingdom and Ireland, an external measure, the British Ability Scales Word Reading Test II (GL Assessment, 2011), is also administered.

The RR intervention is informed by literacy processing theory. Clay (in Doyle, 2013) proposed this theory to explicate the process of learning to read. She drew on cognitive processing theories (cf. Holmes & Singer, 1961; Rumelhart, 2013) to describe change over time in the sources of information that children use and the perceptual and cognitive working systems that they orchestrate as they become literate. As children develop expertise in literacy learning, these working systems self-extend, and children become more capable of completing the increasingly more difficult task of reading and writing continuous texts (Doyle, 2013).

The RR lesson framework, designed to ensure daily coverage of the necessary subcomponents of the strategies employed in a literacy processing model (Clay, 2001, p. 221), involves the rereading of familiar texts, the taking of a Running Record of Text Reading (Clay, 2013) based on a text read the previous day, letter and word work, message writing, and the introduction of a new book.

Factors that potentially moderate the RR effect

One of the key purposes of this meta-analysis was to understand why the estimates of RR vary considerably, not only across primary studies, but across extant meta-analyses. We considered six possible mediating variables: location of the study (United States or outside the United States), study design (experimental or quasi-experimental), the literacy domain of the outcome measures, whether the outcome was from the OSELA or another assessment, the effect of the intervention over time, and whether the effect was based on outcomes that immediately followed the treatment, or if the outcome scores were collected at a second- or third-grade follow-up.

Effectiveness across different literacy domains

According to different theoretical perspectives, skilled reading is a multifaceted process that involves the integration and orchestration of different skills and domains of knowledge. According to Clay (2001), a reader must:

> Draw from all his or her current understanding, and all his or her language competencies, and visual information, and phonological information, and knowledge of printing conventions, in ways which extend both the searching and linking processes as well as the item knowledge repertoires. (Clay, 2001, p. 224)

It is evident, therefore, that different domains must be considered in evaluating the efficacy of a literacy intervention, including, but not limited to, phonemic awareness, phonological awareness, concepts about print, language, spelling, encoding, decoding, comprehension, and observations of the strategic orchestration of these processes.

Phonological awareness is related to later reading achievement (National Institute for Literacy, 2008). Some researchers have queried whether RR is effective in lifting the achievement of struggling readers in this domain. For example, Iversen and Tunmer (1993) compared a modified RR group that received RR plus "explicit code instruction" to both an RR and a comparison group (p. 112). They found that both the modified RR and RR groups reached average levels of performance but that the modified group reached these levels more quickly. Hurry and Sylva (2007) compared RR to a phonological intervention and found that children that received RR improved in terms of literacy learning in a broader array of domains than those in the phonological-intervention group. They also found that the gain of the phonological-intervention group was restricted to the domain of phonological awareness.

The WWC (2013), in its review of RR, found that the intervention had potentially positive effects in terms of alphabetics (including phonemic awareness, letter knowledge, and phonics), reading fluency, and reading comprehension, but that the extent of evidence for all three domains was limited. In terms of general reading achievement, the WWC concluded that the intervention had positive effects but, again, that the extent of the evidence was small.

Literacy involves the integration of a broad range of skills and areas of knowledge. Some researchers have questioned the efficacy of RR in certain domains, and the WWC deemed that the RR had potentially positive or positive effects in different literacy domains, but the extent of evidence was small. We, therefore, suggest that it is critical to parse out the efficacy of the intervention across the different domains that are critical components of literacy learning.

OSELA versus external measures

Some researchers have expressed concern about relying on OSELA-based outcomes to gauge the impact of RR. For example, Hiebert, Colt, Catto, and Gury (1992) questioned the use of the OSELA alone as primary evidence of program effectiveness. Slavin et al. (2011) stated that use of the OSELA is a problem, because its measures are closely aligned to skills taught in RR and that judgment of efficacy on these measures alone could inflate effect-size estimates.

It is not entirely clear if the OSELA is tailored directly to the instructional objectives of RR. The tasks found on the OSELA are not specifically addressed in the lesson framework. For example, the specific words that comprise the Ohio Word test are not directly taught in lessons, and the writing vocabulary task requires children to write as many words as possible in 10 min, which is not an activity that a student would experience in RR lessons. Neither are concepts about print directly taught in RR. The only task that is emphasized or repeated in RR is text reading, but it would be rather difficult to formulate an intervention focused on learning how to read that does not have the child read actual text. Furthermore, it would be difficult to claim that OSELA tasks are unique to RR. Many of the OSELA items are tasks that are commonly found on external measures, including reading words, hearing sounds, identifying letters, writing words, and reading text. One would be hard pressed to argue that interventions provided to comparison students in RR studies do not focus on some or all of those common activities. Larger effect sizes on the OSELA may be more a reflection of an instructionally sensitive and curricular-based measure than a test tailored to the intervention.

Study design

One issue that is frequently raised in extant studies of the efficacy of RR, or indeed any intervention, is the design of such studies, in particular, whether the study is experimental or quasi-experimental. Shanahan and Barr (1995) suggested that many studies published at the time of their review of RR rarely assigned students to a treatment or a comparison group. The WWC (WWC, 2013), in its review of RR, only included three of 79 group design studies that met its evidence standards without reservation. We think it timely, therefore, to conduct a meta-analytic review of the more recent studies (cf. Consortium for Policy Research in Education [CPRE], 2015a; Schwartz, 2005) that adhered to such design standards.

Many meta-analytic reviews apply stringent criteria regarding the acceptance or exclusion of quasi-experiments, the assumption being that randomized experiments can yield unbiased estimates of effect sizes and that effect-size estimates of nonrandomized experiments yield different effects (Shadish, Clarke, & Steiner, 2008). Heinsman and Shadish (1996), however, suggested that if randomized and nonrandomized experiments are equally well designed and executed, they would yield roughly the same effect size. They go on to suggest that when differences occur, researchers should provide separate estimates of treatment effectiveness for the two designs.

Sustainability

One of the most pressing and contentious issues debated in considering the efficacy of RR (or, indeed, any early intervention) is that of the sustainability of gains made by students who participated in the intervention. Given the investment of resources in providing one-to-one literacy support, it seems only appropriate to consider whether children continue to make progress relative to their peers and what their outcomes might have been had they not received an intervention.

Researching continued efficacy of any intervention is difficult, particularly when one tries to attribute causal factors for lost gains. RR is often offered in schools as part of a systemic approach to combat educational disadvantage in areas with high numbers of children experiencing literacy difficulties or who would be classified as being of lower socioeconomic status (cf. Department of Education and Science, 2005; Every Child a Chance Trust, 2009). Evaluations of continued gains are faced with the challenge of accounting for the variety of other factors associated with educational disadvantage and socioeconomic status that influence whether children maintain the academic gains made from an early intervention over time. For example, Lee and Loeb (1995), in a study about the sustained effects of Head Start, found that subsequent schooling of lower quality significantly undermine gains made in high-quality early interventions.

Studies from the United States versus other countries

The first known study of RR was Clay's original field research trial conducted in 1978 (Clay, 2009). There have been a number of additional studies performed to ascertain the effects of the intervention in New Zealand, Australia, the United Kingdom, Canada, and the United States. Apart from Slavin et al. (2011), no researchers have attempted to examine the efficacy of RR by compiling studies from various geographical contexts, and to date, no quantitative review has attempted to ascertain if impact estimates vary significantly across countries. Certain program features do differ across the world. For example, in some countries, the training centers are affiliated with a school district or state ministry of education; in other countries such as the United Kingdom and the United States, training centers are affiliated with universities. Implementation standards vary slightly across nations, and not all countries issue licenses.

Although there are differences in implementation across nations, the theory and general instructional system are quite consistent throughout the world. The International Reading Recovery Trainer Organization provides the opportunity for trainers from different countries to maintain fidelity of implementation. The uniformity in lesson structure and rigorous teaching standards lead us to hypothesize that RR effects are not significantly different across the world.

The United States has had a rich history of producing group comparison studies on RR (see Pinnell, DeFord, & Lyons, 1988), especially experimentally designed studies. In 2010, the U.S. Department of Education awarded The Ohio State University a 5-year multimillion dollar grant to scale up RR. The CPRE at the University of Pennsylvania was contracted to conduct a 4-year independent evaluation of the scale-up, which has led to the largest studies of the intervention to date.

Study purpose

The purpose of this study was to conduct a high-quality meta-analytic review of comparison group studies from across the world about the efficacy of RR. The research questions that guided our inquiry were:
1. What is the overall effect of RR on students' literacy achievement?
2. What factors mediate the immediate, or primary RR effect?
3. What is the sustained effect of RR on students' literacy achievement?

Method

Data sources

We used key terms that allowed us to identify as many studies as possible. Our search terms included: early literacy, early literacy intervention, literacy intervention, primary literacy intervention, first-grade intervention, and RR. A comprehensive review of the literature was conducted utilizing international databases, including EBSCO, PsycInfo, ERIC, Proquest Dissertation Abstracts, DART-Europe E-theses portal, Theses Canada portal, Networked Digital Library of Theses and Dissertations, and WorldCat Dissertations and Theses. We also searched through citations from previous meta-analyses and reviews (D'Agostino & Murphy, 2004; Elbaum et al., 2000; Slavin et al., 2011) and the WWC (2013) intervention report about RR. By e-mail, we contacted researchers and directors of RR training centers in the United Kingdom, Australia, and New Zealand.

Over a year, we collected 203 studies for possible inclusion in this meta-analysis. These included peer-reviewed articles, external evaluations, and 97 doctoral dissertations. Studies ranged from case studies to comparisons of RR to alternate treatments. Each study was allocated a study identification number and catalogued. Each study was read and information about the study design, treatment fidelity, sample size, measures used, and attrition were entered into a database. Many studies lacked a comparison group, or the comparison group could not be considered comparable, or suffered from high attrition, or generally failed to report enough detail to judge study quality. Inclusion in the meta-analysis was based on the fulfillment of the following criteria:

- The treatment group received an RR intervention in any international location;
- Evidence of treatment fidelity;
- Sufficient information was provided to compute effect sizes and effect size weights; and
- In the case of quasi-experimental studies, adjusted means based on covariate analysis were provided, or, if adjusted means were not provided, we utilized the evidence criteria of the WWC (2014) for inclusion of studies in an intervention report. This meant that we calculated whether the differences in mean baseline characteristics of the groups was less than or equal to 5% of the pooled standard deviation of the sample.

Of the vast number of studies that we collated, many were excluded due to the stringent inclusion criteria. For example, a study by Huggins (1999) that had been included in Slavin et al.'s (2011) best-evidence synthesis was excluded, as the author described how the children were enrolled in the intervention for "one full year" (p. i) and provided no information regarding the number of weeks children were in the intervention. As the RR intervention is clearly intended to be a short-term, 20-week intervention, we did not include this study, because it did not fulfill the treatment fidelity criteria.

The number of studies included in the final meta-analysis totaled 16 (see Table 1), 11 of which were conducted in the United States. Two studies were included from the United Kingdom. In addition, there was one study from each of the following countries: Northern Ireland, Australia, and New

Table 1. Summary description of studies.

	Primary Author	Data Collected	Design	Total # RR Students Tested	Location
1	Burroughs-Lange, S.	(2005)	Quasi-experimental	87	United Kingdom
	Burroughs-Lange, S.	(2007)	Quasi-experimental	77	United Kingdom
	Hurry, J.	(2008)	Quasi-experimental	73	United Kingdom
	Hurry, J.	(2010)	Quasi-experimental	77	United Kingdom
2	Hurry, J.	(1992)	Quasi-experimental	95	United Kingdom
3	Clay, M.	(1978)	Quasi-experimental	80	New Zealand
4	Gardner, J.	(1994)	Quasi-experimental	89	Northern Ireland
5	Center, Y.	(1991)	Experimental	31	Australia
6	Huck, C. S.	(1985)	Quasi-experimental	53	USA
	DeFord, D.	(1986)	Quasi-experimental	43	USA
7	Iversen, S.	(1991)	Quasi-experimental	32	USA
8	Pinnell, G. S.	(1985)*	Experimental	131	USA
9	Pinnell, G. S.	(1992)*	Experimental	31	USA
10	Quay, L. C.	(1999)*	Experimental	82	USA
11	Schwartz, R. M.	(2003)	Experimental	37	USA
12	Department of Evaluation Services: Saginaw Public Schools, MI.	(1991)	Quasi-experimental	35	USA
13	CPRE	(2011)	Experimental	431	USA
14	CPRE	(2012)	Experimental	726	USA
15	CPRE	(2013)	Experimental	855	USA
16	CPRE	(2014)	Experimental	1432	USA

Note. RR = Reading Recovery. An asterisk (*) denotes an estimated year.

Zealand. The London Study (Burroughs-Lange & Douetil, 2007) had follow-up studies for treatment and comparison groups at 1, 3 and 5 years after the intervention (Burroughs-Lange, 2008; Hurry, 2012; Hurry & Holliman, 2009). Although published separately, this study was counted as one study, as the research was longitudinal in nature, following the same participants over time. Similarly, the study by DeFord, Pinnell, Lyons, and Young (1987) was a follow-up to the study by Huck and Pinnell (1986) and, thus, they were counted as one study.

The i3 RR grant to scale up RR was conducted over a period of 5 years, with data for 4 years. The first-year results were released as an interim report, as were second-year results in a second interim report. Third- and fourth-year results were reported separately but together in the final report (CPRE did not produce a separate report for the third year of the grant). Schools were randomly chosen to participate in one study year, so the analysis of data each year was based on a new sample of schools. It also needs to be noted that, because the purpose of the scale-up grant was to recruit and train teachers, the great majority of participating teachers were in their training year. If a school already had trained RR teachers, those teachers were allowed to participate, but the majority of teachers were new. Over time, schools from earlier cohorts were sampled to participate, so the results from later years included more trained teachers. The number of teachers with experience, therefore, increased over time as the samples included teachers with schools already trained. Unlike the London study, we treated each i3 evaluation year as a separate study—each year represented different schools, different teachers, and different children.

Of the 16 studies, nine were experimental and seven were quasi-experimental. Of the nine experiments, eight were conducted in the United States, and among the quasi-experiments, three were from the United States. The great majority of experiments were based in the United States, making it difficult to reliably test a study design or U.S. effect.

Chronologically, the studies spanned 36 years, from Clay's 1978 study (in Clay, 2009) to the most recent evaluations of the i3-funded implementation of RR in the United States by CPRE (2013, 2015a, 2015b). Two studies were published in the 1980s, four in the 1990s, six in the 2000s, and four in the 2010s. The most recent four studies, those published in the 2010s, were from the i3 scale-up project.

We entered the following variables into our database: study identification number, study location, whether the study was in the United States or not, year of data collection, year of publication, pre- and posttest means and standard deviations, any follow-up data, name of test, whether the measures used were OSELA (Clay, 2013) or not, and what domain of literacy the measure assessed.

In terms of type of test, there were a total of 56 different literacy assessments used in the various studies. Included in these 56 assessments are the tasks from the OSELA (Clay, 2013). As described previously, we coded whether each assessment was an OSELA task or not. To answer part of our question about what factors mediate the effect of RR, we coded what literacy domain the measure assessed. We coded 11 domains, including encoding, phonological encoding, phonological awareness, decoding, word reading, text reading, listening comprehension, reading comprehension, general literacy, vocabulary, and listening comprehension (see Appendix).

An example of a phonological encoding task is Clay's (2013) *Hearing and recording sounds in words* task. This task measures a child's ability to hear a sound and record an acceptable phoneme even if the spelling is not technically correct (for example, cee/see). In contrast, in an encoding task, like Clay's (2013) *Writing vocabulary* task, only correctly spelling words would receive credit. Tasks were coded as general literacy if they tapped various different domains to receive a total score.

Data analysis

There were 16 studies, with at least one group comparison on an outcome variable. We first computed standardized mean difference effect sizes based on the pooled standard deviation from each group comparison. The effect sizes then were converted to Hedges's *g* values, which corrects for upward bias due to small sample sizes (Hedges, 1981). We then computed variance estimates for each *g* value using conventional procedures, as reported in Shadish and Haddock (1994). Hierarchical linear modeling (HLM) analyses were conducted with the corrected effect sizes serving as the outcome measure and the variance estimates as the weights (hence, an HLM v-known analysis was performed). This is a standard process for meta-analysis as explained by Raudenbush and Bryk (2002).

A two-level HLM model was computed with study as the Level 2 unit. Level 1 consisted of the multiple comparisons per study that were nested in the Level 2 units. We included several variables at Level 1 to examine differential effects by outcome variable type, such as whether the outcome was from OSELA (Clay, 2013) or an external measure. At Level 2, we included two study characteristics, such as whether the study was (a) conducted in the United States or other countries and (2) quasi-experimental or experimental.

Results

In terms of time after the treatment period, there were 101 estimates of the immediate effect of RR across the 16 studies. Our first task was to estimate the overall weighted effect of the intervention immediately after the treatment, and to examine the degree of heterogeneity of those effects. We assumed that the data followed a random effects model (as opposed to a fixed effects model), because the composition and delivery of the intervention likely varied over time, place, and outcome type. Hence, we did not assume that the effects were distributed around one true parameter mean, as is assumed in the fixed effects model. The unconditional HLM model v-known model allowed us to compute an estimate of the overall effect by calculating an average weighted effect for each study, and an overall weighted average of the average study effects. At Level 1, with the 101 individual effects nested within the 16 studies, the overall first-grade effect was .59 ($SE = .09$, 95% CI [.41–.77]). Because zero is not in the confidence interval range, we rejected the null hypothesis that RR does not have an overall effect on student literacy outcomes.

The unconditional model also allowed us to test if the average weighted effects across the 16 studies likely followed a random or fixed effect. The estimate of parameter variance (τ) was .13, and the null hypothesis that $\tau = 0$ was rejected, $\chi^2(15) = 430.32$, $p < .001$, indicating that the degree of heterogeneity around the average effect was substantial enough to warrant a random effects model. Rejection of the null also revealed that HLM was suitable for further data analyses, given that the v-known HLM method follows the procedures for random effects meta-analysis, where the weight of each unique effect is the reciprocal of the effect's variance plus the estimate of τ. HLM also allowed us to examine if certain factors mediated the estimate of the RR effect at Levels 1 and 2.

Factors that moderate the effect of RR

We first examined if the 101 effects varied significantly by the type of literacy domain each effect represented. To do this, we entered dummy variables coded *1* if the outcome represented an effect of a specific domain and *0* for all other effects. We entered the dummy variables as Level 1 predictors because each of the 101 unique effects was derived from a measure that could be categorized into one of the specific literacy domains. We also examined if the average effect sizes differed depending on whether the outcomes were derived from the OSELA or not by including a dummy variable (coded *1* if from the OSELA) at Level 1 in a separate HLM model.

Table 2 presents the results of the Level 1 analyses, along with the overall effect from the unconditional model for comparison purposes. For each variable, the overall weighted effect is provided with the number of effects, and the standard error and 95% confidence interval of the effect estimate. A comparison average effect also is provided, along with a *t*-test result of the comparison between the point estimate and comparison mean value.

The *t*-test for the combined effect examines if the point estimate is significantly different from zero. For the conditional effects, the *t*-test is in comparison to the average of the effect coded *0* for the specific variable. It can be seen that OSELA-based effect yielded a weighted average effect of .79, whereas the non-OSELA effects averaged .45. Because .45 was not in the confidence interval of .67–.91 for OSELA effects, we rejected the null hypothesis that there was no difference between OSELA and non-OSELA effects.

Table 2. Effects of Reading Recovery on literacy achievement.

Outcome	Effect Size	Number of Effects	Standard Error	95% CI	Comparison Mean	t-Value
All combined	.59	101	.09	.41–.77	0	6.61***
Observation Survey of Early Literacy Achievement	.79	45	.06	.67–.91	.45	5.83***
Literacy domains						
Print knowledge	.95	7	.14	.68–1.22	.57	2.72**
Text reading	.84	12	.12	.61–1.08	.55	2.38*
General literacy	.75	15	.04	.67–.83	.55	5.49***
Encoding	.70	8	.11	.48–.92	.58	1.12
Phonological encoding	.70	8	.08	.54–.86	.57	1.68
Phonological awareness	.58	8	.15	.29–.87	.59	.98
Comprehension	.46	12	.02	.42–.50	.61	−6.35**
Word reading	.45	16	.03	.39–.51	.62	−5.95**
Decoding	.45	6	.19	.08–.82	.59	−.76
Letter identification	.33	7	.13	.08–.58	.61	−2.16*
1 effect only:						
Vocabulary	−.14	1	.16	−.45–.17	.59	−4.53***
Listening comprehension	1.09	1	.17	.59–1.42	.76	3.00***

Note. *p < .05. **p < .01. ***p < .001.

The largest effects were for measures of print knowledge (for example, concepts about print; .95, SE = .14, 95% CI [.68–1.22]) and text reading (for example, text reading level; .84, SE = .12, 95% CI [.61–1.08]; see Figure 1). These results indicate that RR has a positive effect on these broad, more direct indicators of text reading. There were lower effects for comprehension and word reading. Nonetheless, because zero was not included in the confidence intervals for both effect estimates, there were positive effects for both domains. The lowest effect was for letter identification (.33, SE = .13, 95% CI [.08–

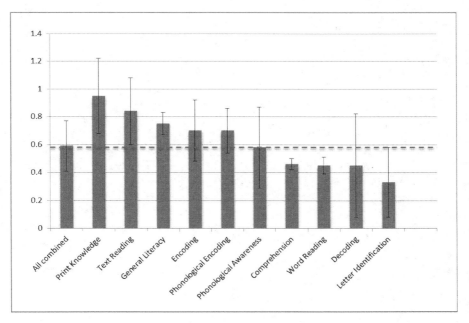

Figure 1. Reading Recovery effects by literacy domain.

.58]). Given that in first grade, however, many children would know most of their letters, there perhaps was not room for a significant effect in this domain to be evident.

The effect of RR on general literacy (which included 15 non-OSELA measures of literacy achievement) was high at .75 ($SE = .04$, 95% CI [.67–.83]). The results obtained for vocabulary and listening comprehension are only included to account for all 101 effects. The results for both domains should be treated with caution, as there was only one effect for both domains.

We also discovered, however, that domains with above average effects tended to be based on OSELA outcomes, and domains with lower than average effects tended to be based on non-OSELA measures. All seven print knowledge effects were OSELA-based measures, as were all eight of the phonological encoding measures. For text reading, 75% (9 of 12) of the effects were from the OSELA, and 88% of the encoding effects were OSELA-based. For lower than average domains, comprehension and decoding were comprised of no OSELA measures, and 38% (6 of 16) of the word reading effects were from the OSELA. Letter identification, however, was entirely based on the OSELA letter identification task, but it is known to have a ceiling effect among first-grade students, which likely explained the lower than average effect for that domain. For the other domains, we surmised that at least some of the effect differential may have resulted from an OSELA confound.

To test our assumption, we controlled for whether the measures were OSELA or not by adding the dummy variable as a Level 1 covariate. Adding the OSELA dummy variable had no bearing on the average effect for print knowledge, text reading, comprehension, word reading, and letter identification. The effects for encoding and phonological encoding, however, were no different than the overall average of .58 after controlling for OSELA. The effect for decoding also was no different from the overall average after the adjustment.

We analyzed three Level 2 predictors (United States or outside United States; experiment or quasi-experiment; and years since the study was conducted, coded *0* for the first study in 1978). We entered each as a single Level 2 predictor of the study intercepts, which reflects the average effect from each study. None of the three variables were significant. Although U.S. studies tended to yield larger average effects (there was a .09 effect difference in favor of U.S. studies), the standard error was too large (.20) to produce a significant *t*-value. Experiments also tended to yield larger effects than quasi-experiments (the difference was .26), but, given the standard error of .19, the difference was not significant. Again, because seven of the eight experiments were conducted in the United States, it was difficult to ascertain the unique contribution of either variable. The effect size change per year was virtually zero (.01, $SE = .01$), and thus was not significant (see Figure 2).

Table 3 presents the results of two HLM Level 2 analyses. Model 1 includes all three variables as predictors of the study intercepts, or average effect size per study. As can be seen, none of the three variables included simultaneously as potential predictors were significant. Because the variables were uncentered, the intercept of 0.37 indicates the estimated average effect for a non-U.S. study, quasi-experiment, conducted in the first publication year, 1978 (all variables coded 0). Model 2 includes the prediction of the difference between OSELA and non-OSELA effects within each of the studies. It can be seen that experimentally based studies produced larger effect differences (of the magnitude of .45) for OSELA effects compared to non-OSELA effects. Also note that, over time, the difference in OSELA versus non-OSELA effects within studies grew by a magnitude of .02 per year. Thus, over each 10-year period, studies tended to produce .20 larger effects for OSELA-based measures compared to non-OSELA measures. U.S. studies did not demonstrate any difference in OSELA versus non-OSELA effects.

To examine further the widened gap over time for OSELA and non-OSELA measures, we conducted follow-up HLM analyses based on effects produced by each set of outcomes separately. We included the other two Level 2 predictors in each model. For the non-OSELA measures, *years since first study* did not predict effect sizes ($\gamma_{03} = .01$, $SE = .01$, $t(6) = .52$), but, for OSELA measures, the time variable was a significant positive predictor. On OSELA measures, the average effect increased by .04 ($SE = .01$) per year, $t(6) = 5.53$, $p < .001$. The gap increased over time, evidently, because the effects on OSELA measures increased while the effects on non-OSELA measures remained stable.

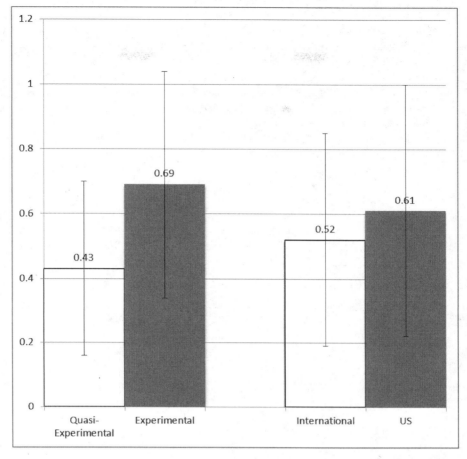

Figure 2. Comparison of effects of quasi-experimental versus experimental and international or U.S. studies of Reading Recovery.

The sustained effect of RR on students' literacy achievement

Four studies provided six Grade 2 effect-size estimates. Three of the four studies with second-grade follow-up effects also yielded third-grade effects. One other study provided third-grade follow-up effects but no second-grade effect estimates. There were 10 unique effects across the four

Table 3. Hierarchical linear modeling results for level 2 predictors.

Fixed Effect	Model 1	Model 2
For Intercept, β_0		
Intercept, γ_{00}	0.37(0.20)1.87	0.46(0.21)2.19*
United States, γ_{01}	−0.08(0.24)−0.34	−0.06(0.24)−0.23
Experiment, γ_{02}	0.22(0.24)0.91	0.06(0.24)0.26
Years since first study, γ_{03}	0.01(0.01)0.68	0.01(0.01)0.54
For Observation Survey of Early Literacy Achievement slope, β_1		
Intercept, γ_{10}	—	−0.36(0.20)−1.82
United States, γ_{11}	—	−0.05(0.10)−0.49
Experiment, γ_{12}	—	0.45(0.09)5.07***
Years since first study, γ_{13}	—	0.02(0.01)3.36**

Note. ***$p < .001$. **$p < .01$. *$p < .05$. Values in cells represent coefficients (SE) and t-ratios.

studies with third-grade data. We followed the same HLM procedures for computing the primary effects, but, due to the small number of studies with follow-up effects, we did not attempt to examine the potential impact of Level 2 moderating variables. Instead, separate unconditional models were created to estimate the second- and third-grade follow-up effects.

The average weighted second-grade random effect was .30 ($SE = .26$; 95% CI [−.21–.81]), and the average weighted random effect at third grade was −.01 ($SE = .21$; 95% CI [−.42–.40]). In both cases, the 95% confidence intervals contained zero, indicating that the null hypotheses of no sustained second- or third-grade effects could not be rejected.

For the sustained effects estimates to represent a valid inference regarding the longer term impact of the intervention, it was imperative to document the estimated primary, or immediate, effect of the subsample of studies that provided second- or third-grade follow-up results. Among the four studies that examined second-grade impacts, the primary weighted random effect estimate from those studies was .53. Although that point estimate was lower than the overall weighted random effect of .59, it was within the 95% confidence interval of the overall effect, indicating that the difference between point estimates likely was due to sampling error. The immediate effect of the subsample of studies with third-grade follow-up data, however, was .30, which is outside the 95% confidence interval of the overall immediate effect, and thus, it could not be concluded that studies with third-grade follow-up effects were representative of studies with primary effects.

Discussion

RR is one of the most researched early literacy interventions in the world. To date, there have been four quantitative syntheses that were designed to ascertain the impact of the intervention. Although all of the former meta-analyses have drawn positive conclusions about RR, the estimated overall effect has varied across the studies due to certain design features, available studies at the time of the synthesis, and scope of the study.

By selecting rigorously designed experiments or quasi-experiments conducted worldwide over the entire span of RR, we estimated the overall effect to be slightly higher (.59) than the average of the prior studies (.54). As is the case in all quantitative syntheses, a vital question is: What is the magnitude of the overall effect? According to Cohen's (1988) guidelines, the effect would be considered medium, but, as is commonly known, Cohen did not produce his guidelines to be aligned with what is normative for educational interventions (Lipsey et al., 2012). The WWC identified 26 early literacy interventions that had sufficient evidence to produce reliable effect estimates. Among those interventions, the first author (D'Agostino & Brownfield, 2015) computed an overall g-corrected effect of .34 ($SD = .20$), which included the WWC estimate of .70 on a smaller set of studies. The .59 overall effect found in this study would place RR at about the 89th percentile in the WWC distribution of early literacy interventions implemented in the United States. The .61 effect for U.S. studies included in this meta-analysis would place RR at the 91st percentile in the WWC distribution (the .70 effect found for RR by the WWC placed the intervention at the 96th percentile in the WWC distribution). RR clearly is in the upper echelon in terms of overall impact among interventions targeted for beginning readers.

The estimate of RR impact, however, depends to a great extent on the literacy domain the outcomes represent. The intervention produced larger effect estimates on measures of print knowledge, text reading, encoding, and phonological encoding. It produced average effects on measures of phonological awareness, and smaller than average effects on comprehension, word reading, decoding, and letter identification.

Given that the RR intervention involves daily reading of continuous text, we suggest that it is not surprising that the intervention had larger effects on measures of text reading and print knowledge. Children that receive the intervention engage in daily reading of approximately two to four little books and engage in the writing of continuous texts. Over the course of the intervention, therefore, children are afforded the opportunity to read and write a vast volume of texts that could, in turn, produce larger effects in the domains of text reading and concepts about print, especially when compared to children in alternate treatments.

RR also involves daily writing of an authentic message that involves the processes of encoding (spelling) and phonological encoding. In particular, large effects in these domains may be due to an instructional emphasis on spelling and teaching children how to hear and record sounds in words. An alternative explanation may be that the larger effect estimates in these domains may be confounded with the fact that, for the majority of studies, the encoding and phonological encoding measures were the *writing vocabulary* and *hearing and recording sounds in words* tasks from the OSELA. We could not rule out that alternative explanation, because the moderating effects on the two encoding domains were nullified once we controlled for OSELA or non-OSELA measures.

The intervention produced average effects on measures of phonological awareness and smaller than average effects on measures of decoding, which echoes the finding of Iversen and Tunmer (1993) and Hurry and Sylva (2007). It is also likely that, because the instruction and intervention that control children were receiving in these studies placed a strong instructional emphasis on decoding, the RR effect would shrink in these domains.

There was a smaller than average effect for letter identification. This is not surprising because, as Paris (2005) stated, letter knowledge is a constrained skill. In effect, by first grade many children know most of their letters and, thus, there is little room for growth in this domain. The relatively diminutive effect on comprehension measures is not uncommon for beginning reading interventions. D'Agostino and Brownfield (2015) found that beginning reading programs with WWC reviews had an overall comprehension effect of .19.

Researchers such as Hiebert et al. (1992) and Slavin et al. (2011) have argued that effect estimates based on the OSELA are biased, because the tasks in it are tailored to the intervention. We did find that OSELA-based measures yielded significantly larger effects (nearly 0.80) than non-OSELA measures. We also found that the OSELA effect increased over time, but the non-OSELA effect remained constant. It could be argued that the latter finding is congruent with the position that OSELA outcomes produce biased estimates, perhaps due to teaching to the test, which has led to the intervention, over time, becoming more focused on addressing the particular content of the OSELA tasks.

Yet the OSELA tasks are not unique to RR and, generally, are the types of items found on many literacy assessments. The tasks consist of activities such as letter naming, generating words, reading words, reading print, and identifying and hearing sounds in words, many of which are activities commonly found on other curricular-based measures. A rival interpretation of the larger effect for OSELA may be that it is a more instructionally sensitive measure that is targeted at the lower end of the distribution of early readers than many standardized tests. So it is possible that the observed OSELA-based effects more closely approximate the true literacy achievement parameter effect. Under this particular perspective, the effect gap over time may reveal that RR, indeed, has become more effective, but the increased effectiveness is only detectable on more instructionally sensitive indicators.

We also examined whether studies conducted in the United States yielded different effect estimates from studies in other countries, and if experiments produced different effect estimates from quasi-experiments. We discovered that the two variables dramatically overlapped, with 87% of the experiments being conducted in the United States. Neither variable, alone or considered simultaneously, predicted effects. Although the point estimates were greater for U.S. studies and for experiments, the standard errors were too large to reject the null hypotheses. Given the relatively small number of studies, however, it is possible that lack of statistical power delimited our capacity to detect statistically significant differences. The inclusion of more studies over time may allow for better estimates of method effects or international comparisons. Based on our findings, we concluded that RR has not been more effective in the United States, and that experiments and quasi-experiments tend to yield similar program effect estimates.

Since its inception in the late 1970s in New Zealand, the effects of RR on student literacy achievement have been rather stable. When we combined OSELA and non-OSELA effects (and for non-OSELA effects only), the estimate of treatment impact has been similar up to and including the i3 external evaluation. Because the goal of the i3 project was to recruit new teachers to offer RR, there were a disproportionate number of novice teachers in the study. The disproportion likely was present in Clay's original study because teachers were working with an innovative approach to literacy teaching. The remaining studies likely contained samples of teachers with more experience, on average. The lack of change in effect over time may reflect the stability of the intervention to produce strong results even with fluctuations in the delivery system, such as the experience level of teachers. The stability may be a key reason that RR has remained at scale worldwide for four decades.

The results of the follow-up analysis are inconclusive, but slightly more informative for second-grade than for third-grade children. Our best inference is that, by second grade, the immediate effect of .59 appears to diminish to .30. However, with only four studies and six unique effects, the estimation error was too large to conclude that a sustained effect occurs at all. The results for third grade are more tenuous: The point estimate of a third-grade sustained effect was near zero, but the small sample size coupled with the nonrepresentative primary effects from the subsample of studies rendered the estimate of a null third-grade effect practically meaningless.

Given that a primary goal of RR is to identify children who would benefit most from special education, the intent-to-treat model of most impact studies does not allow a more complete inquiry into the positive consequences of the intervention. The expectation in RR is that some children will not respond positively to the treatment, and, thus, there is no further assumption that referred children will catch their average performing peers due to RR participation, in the short or long term.

For the child who does respond favorably to RR, it remains debatable if an intervention designed to recover the child's literacy growth trajectory should be held accountable for his or her achievement 2 or 3 years beyond the intervention period. RR is a short-term intervention meant to be integrated into a schooling system with other interventions and regular classroom practice that should work in unison to promote sustained growth. Once a child is successfully exited from RR, the child should be no more vulnerable to poor classroom instruction and life circumstances than any other average achieving child. RR alone in first grade, however, does not solve the exogenous circumstances that likely contributed to reading difficulties in the first place, such as poverty, language issues in the home, community problems, or poor schooling in underprivileged neighborhoods. The findings of this study and other studies of RR impact consistently have demonstrated that with effective literacy instruction, at-risk children can beat the odds and accelerate their achievement gains. But to the extent that the exogenous conditions persist (and they surely do), then it is likely that they will continue to complicate students' academic success over time, as was discovered in the examination of immediate and long-term Head Start effects (Lee & Loeb, 1995).

In conducting this meta-analysis of RR, we have attempted to address gaps in extant research by including recent studies from around the world and by applying stringent inclusion criteria. In addition to analyzing the efficacy of the intervention, we have considered the variation around the effect and where these effects are sustained. Our results demonstrate that RR is, indeed, an effective early literacy intervention for struggling readers, regardless of educational context.

References[1]

*Burroughs-Lange, S. (2008). *Comparison of literacy progress of young children in London Schools: A RR Follow-Up Study*. London, UK: Institute of Education. Retrieved from https://www.ioe.ac.uk/Comparison_of_Literacy_Progress_of_Young_Children_in_London_Schools_-_A_Reading_Recovery_Follow_up_Study_.pdf

*Burroughs-Lange, S., & Douetil, J. (2007). Literacy progress of young children from poor urban settings: A Reading Recovery comparison study. *Literacy Teaching and Learning, 12*(1), 19–46. Retrieved from https://readingrecovery.org/images/pdfs/Journals/LTL/LTL_Vol12_No1-2007/LTL_12.1-Burroughs-Lange-Douetil.pdf

*Center, Y., Wheldall, K., Freeman, L., Outhred, L., & McNaught, M. (1995). An evaluation of Reading Recovery. *Reading Research Quarterly, 30*, 240–263. doi: 10.2307/748034

Clay, M. M. (2001). *Change over time in children's literacy development*. Auckland, NZ: Heinemann Educational.

*Clay, M. M. (2009). The development project. In B. Watson & B. Askew (Eds.), *Boundless Horizons*. Rosedale, North Shore, NZ: Heinemann.

Clay, M. M. (2013). *An observation survey of early literacy achievement*. Portsmouth, NH: Heinemann.

Cohen, J. (1988). *Statistical power analysis for the behavioral sciences* (2nd ed.). Hillsdale, NJ: Lawrence Erlbaum.

---

[1] *denotes study included in final meta-analytic review.

*Consortium for Policy Research in Education. (2013). *Evaluation of the i3 scale up of Reading Recovery: Year One report 2011–2012.* Philadelphia, PA: University of Pennsylvania. Retrieved from http://www.cpre.org/evaluation-i3-scale-reading-recovery-year-one-report-2011-12

*Consortium for Policy Research in Education. (2015a). *Evaluation of the i3 scale up of Reading Recovery: Year Two report 2012–2013.* Philadelphia, PA: University of Pennsylvania. Retrieved from http://www.cpre.org/rryr2

*Consortium for Policy Research in Education. (2015b). *Evaluation of the i3 scale up of Reading Recovery: Years Three and Four report 2013–2015.* Philadelphia, PA: University of Pennsylvania.

D'Agostino, J. V., & Brownfield, K. (April, 2015). *A closer look at what works: Theoretical and instructional perspectives behind beginning reading interventions.* Paper presented at the meeting of the American Educational Research Association, Chicago, IL.

D'Agostino, J. V., & Harmey, S. (2014). *Reading Recovery and Descubriendo la Lectura National Report 2013–2014.* Columbus, OH: International Data Evaluation Center. Retrieved from https://www.idecweb.us/Publications.aspx

D'Agostino, J. V., & Murphy, J. A. (2004). A meta-analysis of Reading Recovery in United States schools. *Educational Evaluation and Policy Analysis, 26*(1), 23–38. doi: 10.3102/01623737026001023

*DeFord, D., Pinnell, G. S., Lyons, C. A., & Young, P. (1987). *Reading Recovery program: Report of the follow-up studies (Vol. VII).* Columbus, OH: The Ohio State University.

Department of Education and Science. (2005). *DEIS: Delivering equality of opportunity in Schools.* Dublin, Ireland: Department of Education and Science, Ireland.

*Department of Evaluation Services. (1995). *Compensatory education (CE) product evaluation: Elementary and secondary programs 1994–95.* Saginaw, MI: Saginaw Public Schools. (ERIC Document Reproduction Service No. ED391853).

Doyle, M. A. (2013). Marie M. Clay's theoretical perspective: A literacy processing theory. In D. E. Alvermann, N. Unrau, & R. B. Ruddell (Eds.), *Theoretical models and processes of reading, sixth edition* (pp. 636–656). Newark, DE: International Reading Association.

Elbaum, B., Vaughn, S., Hughes, M., & Moody, S. (2000). How effective are one-to-one tutoring programs in reading for elementary students at risk of reading failure? A meta-analysis of the intervention research. *Journal of Educational Psychology, 92*, 605–619. doi: 10.1037//0022-0663.92.4.605

Every Child a Chance Trust. (2009). *The long term costs of literacy difficulties* (2d ed.). Retrieved from https://www.kpmg.com/UK/en/IssuesAndInsights/ArticlesPublications/Documents/PDF/What%20We%20Do/ecc-long_term_costs_of_literacy_report_2nd_edition.pdf

*Gardner, J., Sutherland, A., & Meenan-Strain, C. (1998) *Reading Recovery in Northern Ireland: The first two years.* Belfast, Ireland: Blackstaff.

GL Assessment (2011). *BAS II Word Reading Scale.* London, UK: GL Education Group.

Hedges, L. V. (1981). Distribution theory for Glass's estimator of effect size and related estimators. *Journal of Educational Statistics, 6*, 107–128. doi: 10.2307/1164588

Heinsman, D. T., & Shadish, W. R. (1996). Assignment methods in experimentation: When do nonrandomized experiments approximate answers from randomized experiments? *Psychological Methods, 1*, 154–169. doi: 10.1037/1082-989x.1.2.154

Hiebert, E. H., Colt, J. M., Catto, S. L., & Gury, E. C. (1992). Reading and writing of first-grade students in a restructured Chapter 1 program. *American Educational Research Journal, 29*, 545–572. doi: 10.3102/0002831202900354

Holmes, J. A., & Singer, H. (1961). *The substrata-factor theory: Substrata factor differences underlying reading ability in known-groups at the high school level.* Berkeley, CA: University of California.

*Huck, C. S., & Pinnell, G. S (1986). *The Reading Recovery Project in Columbus, Ohio, Vol.1 Pilot year 1984–1985.* Columbus, OH: The Ohio State University.

Huggins, R. (1999). *Longitudinal study of the Reading Recovery program: 1994–1998.* Detroit, MI: Detroit Public Schools, Office of Research, Evaluation, and Assessment. (ERIC Document Reproduction Service No. ED 430067).

*Hurry, J. (2012). *The impact of Reading Recovery five years after intervention.* London, UK: University of London, Institute of Education. Retrieved from http://www.ioe.ac.uk/Research_Home/Hurry-London-Follow-Up-2012-Report-December.pdf

*Hurry, J., & Holliman, A. (2009). *The impact of Reading Recovery three years after intervention.* London, UK: University of London, Institute of Education. Retrieved from https://www.ioe.ac.uk/PHD_JH_Reading_Recovery_report_2009.pdf

*Hurry, J., & Sylva, K. (2007). Long-term outcomes of early reading intervention. *Journal of Reading Research, 30*, 227–248. doi: 10.1111/j.1467-9817.2007.00338.x

*Iversen, S., & Tunmer, W. E. (1993). Phonological processing skills and the Reading Recovery program. *Journal of Educational Psychology, 85*, 112–126. doi: 10.1037/0022-0663.85.1.112

Juel, C. (1988). Learning to read and write: A longitudinal study of 54 children from first through fourth grades. *Journal of Educational Psychology, 80*, 437–447. doi: 10.1037/0022-0663.80.4.437

Lee, V. E., & Loeb, S. (1995). Where do Head Start attendees end up? One reason why preschool effects fade out. *Educational Evaluation and Policy Analysis, 17*, 62–82. doi: 10.3102/01623737017001062

Lipsey, M. W., Puzio, K., Yun, C., Hebert, M. A., Steinka-Fry, K., Cole, M. W., … Busick, M. D. (2012). *Translating the statistical representation of the effects of education interventions into more readily interpretable forms.* (NCSER

2013–3000). Washington, DC: National Center for Special Education Research, Institute of Education Sciences, U.S. Department of Education.

National Institute for Literacy. (2008). *Developing early literacy: Report of the National Early Literacy Panel*. Jessup, MD: National Institute for Literacy.

Paris, S. G. (2005). Reinterpreting the development of reading skills. *Reading Research Quarterly, 40*, 184–202. doi:10.1598/RRQ.40.2.3

*Pinnell, G. S., DeFord, D. E., & Lyons, C. A. (1988). *Reading Recovery: Early intervention for at-risk first graders (Educational Research Service Monograph)*. Arlington, VA: Educational Research Service. (ERIC Document Reproduction Service No. ED303790).

*Pinnell, G. S., Lyons, C. A., Deford, D. E., Bryk, A. S., & Selzer, M. (1994). Comparing instructional models for the literacy education of high-risk first graders. *Reading Research Quarterly, 29*, 8–39. doi: 10.2307/747736

*Quay, L. C., Steele, D. D., Johnson, C. I., & Hortman, W. (2001). Children's achievement and personal and social development in a first-year Reading Recovery program with teachers in training. *Literacy Teaching and Learning: An International Journal of Early Reading and Writing, 5*(2), 7–25. Retrieved from https://readingrecovery.org/images/pdfs/Journals/LTL/LTL_Vol5_No2-2001/LTL_5.2-Quay-Steele-etal.pdf

Raudenbush, S. W., & Bryk, A. S. (2002). *Hierarchical linear models: Applications and data analysis methods (2nd ed.)*. Thousand Oaks, CA: Sage.

Reynolds, M., Wheldall, K., & Madelaine, A. (2010). Components of effective early reading interventions for young struggling readers. *Australian Journal of Learning Difficulties, 15*, 171–192. doi: 10.1080/19404150903579055

Rumelhart, D. E. (2013). Toward an interactive model of reading. In D. E. Alvermann, N. Unrau, & R. B. Ruddell (Eds.), *Theoretical models and processes of reading, sixth edition* (pp. 636–656). Newark, DE: International Reading Association.

*Schwartz, R. M. (2005). Literacy learning of at-risk first-grade students in the Reading Recovery Early Intervention. *Journal of Educational Psychology, 97*, 257–267. doi: 10.1037/0022-0663.97.2.257

Scull, J. A., & Lo Bianco, J. (2008). Successful engagement in an early literacy intervention. *Journal of Early Childhood Literacy, 8*, 123–150. doi: 10.1177/1468798408091852.

Shadish, W. R., Clark, M. H., & Steiner, P. M. (2008). Can nonrandomized experiments yield accurate answers? A randomized experiment comparing random and nonrandom experiments. *Journal of the American Statistical Association, 103*, 1334–1356. doi:10.1198/016214508000000733.

Shadish, W. R., & Haddock, C. K. (1994). Combining estimates of effect size. In H. Cooper & L. V. Hedges (Eds.), *Handbook of research synthesis* (pp. 261–281). New York, NY: Russell Sage Foundation.

Shanahan, T., & Barr, R. (1995). Reading Recovery: An independent evaluation of the effects of an early instructional intervention for at-risk learners. *Reading Research Quarterly, 30*, 958–996. doi:10.2307/748206

Slavin, R., Lake, C., Davis, S., & Madden, N. (2011). Effective programs for struggling readers: A best-evidence synthesis. *Educational Research Review, 6*, 1–26. doi: 10.1016/j.edurev.2010.07.002

Stanovich, K. E. (1986). Matthew effects in reading: Some consequences of individual differences in the acquisition of literacy. *Reading Research Quarterly, 21*, 360–407. doi: 10.1598/rrq.21.4.1

Vellutino, F. R. (2010). "Learning to be learning disabled": Marie Clay's seminal contribution to the response to intervention approach to identifying specific reading disability. *Journal of Reading Recovery, 10*(1), 5–23. Retrieved from https://readingrecovery.org/images/pdfs/Journals/JRR/Vol10_No1_Fall-2010/JRR_10.1_Vellutino.pdf

Vellutino, F. R., & Scanlon, D. (2003). Emergent literacy skills, early instruction, and individual differences as determinants of difficulties in learning to read: The case for early intervention. In S. Neuman & D. Dickinson. (Eds.), *The handbook of early literacy research* (pp. 295–321). New York, NY: Guildford.

What Works Clearinghouse, U.S. Department of Education, Institute of Education Sciences, National Center for Education Evaluation and Regional Assistance (2013*). Beginning reading intervention report: Reading Recovery*. Retrieved from http://ies.ed.gov/ncee/wwc/interventionreport.aspx?sid=420

What Works Clearinghouse, U.S. Department of Education, Institute of Education Sciences, National Center for Education Evaluation and Regional Assistance (2014). *Procedures and standards handbook (version 3.0)*. Retrieved from http://ies.ed.gov/ncee/wwc/DocumentSum.aspx?sid=19

Appendix

	Primary Author	Measures Used/ Current Reference	Type of Measure
1	Burroughs-Lange, S. (2007) Burroughs-Lange, S. (2008) Hurry, J. (2009) Hurry, J. (2011)	1. Letter Identification (Clay, 2013) 2. Hearing and Recording Sounds in Words (Clay, 2013) 3. Writing Vocabulary (Clay, 2013) 4. Concepts About Print (Clay, 2013) 5. Text Reading Level (Clay, 2013) 6. WRAPS Age (Moseley, 2003) 7. BAS Word Reading Age (Elliott, 1996) 8. UK National Curriculum Reading (in Hurry & Holliman, 2009) 9. UK National Curriculum Writing (in Hurry & Holliman, 2009)	Letter ID Phonological encoding Encoding Concepts about print Text reading Decoding Word reading General literacy General literacy
2	Center, Y. (1995)	1. Waddington Diagnostic Spelling Test (Waddington, N., 2000) 2. Treiman Syllable Comparison (cited in Center et al.,1995) 3. Phonemic Awareness Test (Macquarie University Special Education Centre, no reference provided) 4. BURT Word Reading Test (Gilmore, Croft, & Reid, 1981) 5. Text Reading Level (Clay, 2013) 6. Passage Reading Test (cited in Center et al., 1985) 7. Neale Assessment of Reading Ability (1988) 8. Cloze Test (Macquarie University Special Education Centre, no reference) 9. Word Attack Skills Test (Macquarie University Special Education Centre, no reference)	Encoding Phonological awareness Phonological awareness Word reading Text reading Text reading Reading comprehension Reading comprehension Decoding
3	Clay, M. (2009)	1. Hearing and Recording Sounds in Words (Clay, 2013) 2. Writing Vocabulary (Clay, 2013) 3. Concepts about Print (Clay, 2013) 4. Duncan Word Test (Clay, 2013) 5. Text Reading Level (Clay, 2013) 6. Letter Identification (Clay, 2013)	Phonological encoding Encoding Concepts about print Word reading Text reading Letter identification
4	Gardner, J. (1998)	1. MacMillan Individual Reading Analysis Test: Accuracy (Vincent & De La Mare, 1990) 2. MacMillan Individual Reading Analysis Test: Comprehension 3. MacMillan Individual Reading Analysis Test: Errors	Text reading Reading comprehension Text reading
5	Hurry, J. (2007)	1. Oddities Test (Kirtley, Bryant, Maclean, & Bradley, 1989) 2. British Ability Scales Word Reading Age (Elliott, Murray, & Pearson, 1984) 3. Text Reading Level (Clay, 2013) 4. Neale Analysis of Reading Ability (Neale, 1988) 5. OSELA Z-Scores (Clay, 2013) 6. NFER-Nelson Group Reading Test 6-12 (NFER-Nelson, 1985) 7. Parallel Spelling Test (Young, 1983) 8. Overall Reading and Spelling (NFER + Parallel summed and transformed to z)	Phonological awareness Word reading Text reading Reading comprehension General literacy General literacy Encoding General literacy
6	Huck, C. S. (1986)	1. Hearing and Recording Sounds in Words (Clay, 2013) 2. Writing Vocabulary (Clay, 2013) 3. Columbus Study Phonetic Dictation (cited in DeFord et al., 1987) 4. Columbus Study Spelling Accuracy (cited in DeFord et al., 1987) 5. Concepts about Print (Clay, 2013) 6. Stanford Word Study Skills (The Psychological Corporation, 1983)	Phonological encoding Encoding Phonological encoding Encoding Concepts about print Decoding

(Continued)

	Primary Author	Measures Used/ Current Reference	Type of Measure
		7. Ohio Word Test (Clay, 2013)	Word reading
		8. Stanford Word Reading (The Psychological Corporation, 1983)	Word reading
		9. Text Reading Level (Clay, 2013)	Text reading
		10. ITBS NPR Comprehension (cited in Huck & Pinnell, 1986)	General literacy
		11. Stanford Reading Sub-total (The Psychological Corporation, 1983)	General literacy
		12. Letter Identification (Clay, 2013).	Letter identification
		13. Stanford Reading Total (The Psychological Corporation, 1983	General literacy
7	Iversen, S.	1. Concepts about print (Clay, 2013)	Concepts about print
		2. Writing Vocabulary (Clay, 2013)	Encoding
		3. Letter identification (Clay, 2013)	Letter identification
		4. Hearing and recording sounds in words (Clay, 2013)	Phonological encoding
		5. Text reading level (Clay, 2013)	Text reading
		6. Dolch word test (Dolch, 1948)	Word reading
		7. Yopp-Singer phoneme segmentation (Yopp, 1995)	Phonological awareness
		8. Yopp-Singer phoneme deletion (Yopp, 1995)	Phonological awareness
		9. Yopp-Singer phoneme recoding (Yopp, 1995)	Phonological awareness
8	Pinnell, G. S. (1988)	1. Concepts about print (Clay, 2013)	Concepts about print
		2. Hearing and recording sounds in words (Clay, 2013)	Phonological encoding
		3. Letter identification (Clay, 2013)	Letter identification
		4. Ohio word test (Clay, 2013)	Word test
		5. Text reading level (Clay, 2013)	Text reading
		6. Writing vocabulary (Clay, 2013)	Encoding
9	Pinnell, G. S. (1994)	1. Gates MacGinitie Reading Test (MacGinitie et al., 2000)	General literacy
		2. Hearing and recording sounds in words (Clay, 2013)	Encoding
		3. Mason early reading test (Mason & McCormick, 1984)	General literacy
		4. Text reading level (Clay, 2013)	Text reading
		5. Woodcock reading mastery (Woodcock, 1987)	General literacy
10	Quay, L. C. (2001)	1. ITBS language total (Hoover, Dunbar, & Frisbie, 2000)	General literacy
		2. ITBS reading comprehension (Hoover, Dunbar, & Frisbie, 2000)	Reading comprehension
		3. ITBS listening (Hoover, Dunbar, & Frisbie, 2000)	Listening comprehension
		4. ITBS reading total (Hoover, Dunbar, & Frisbie, 2000)	General literacy
		5. ITBS vocabulary (Hoover, Dunbar, & Frisbie, 2000)	Vocabulary
		6. ITBS word analysis (Hoover, Dunbar, & Frisbie, 2000)	Decoding
		7. Letter identification (Clay, 2013)	Letter identification
		8. Ohio word test (Clay, 2013)	Word reading
		9. Text reading level (Clay, 2013)	Text reading
		10. Writing vocabulary (Clay, 2013)	Encoding
11	Schwartz, R. M. (2005)	1. Concepts about Print (Clay, 2013)	Concepts about print
		2. Degrees of reading power (Touchstone, 2000)	General literacy
		3. Hearing and recording sounds in words (Clay, 2013)	Phonological encoding
		4. Letter identification (Clay, 2013)	Letter identification
		5. Ohio word test (Clay, 2013)	Word reading
		6. SORT 3-R (Slosson, 2007)	Word reading
		7. Text reading level (Clay, 2013)	Text reading
		8. Writing vocabulary (Clay, 2013)	Encoding
		9. Yopp-Singer phoneme deletion (Yopp, 1995)	Phonological awareness
		10. Yopp- Singer phoneme segmentation (Yopp, 1995)	Phonological awareness
12	Department of Evaluation Services, Saginaw Public Schools, MI. (1995)	1. Hearing and recording sounds in words (Clay, 2013)	Phonological encoding
13-16	Consortium for Policy Research in Education (2013, 2015a, 2015b)	1. ITBS Reading Comprehension (Hoover, Dunbar, & Frisbie, 2000)	Reading comprehension
		2. ITBS Reading Total (Hoover, Dunbar, & Frisbie, 2000)	General literacy
		3. ITBS Reading Words (Hoover, Dunbar, & Frisbie, 2000)	Word reading
		4. OSELA Total Score (D'Agostino, 2012)	General literacy

Reading Recovery: Exploring the Effects on First-Graders' Reading Motivation and Achievement

Celeste C. Bates, Jerome V. D'Agostino, Linda Gambrell, and Menglin Xu

ABSTRACT

This study examined the effects of Reading Recovery on children's motivational levels, and how motivation may contribute to the effect of the intervention on literacy achievement. Prior studies concluded that Reading Recovery was positively associated with increased student motivation levels, but most of those studies were limited methodologically. The achievement and motivation levels before and after the intervention of Reading Recovery students and similarly low-performing first-grade students were compared using structural equation modeling. It was found that Reading Recovery had a .31 treatment effect on achievement after controlling for baseline achievement and motivational differences among the treatment and comparison students. Reading Recovery also was associated with greater average levels of posttest motivation, and motivation was found to mediate the treatment-achievement relationship. This study highlights how important it is for early reading interventions to consider the role motivation plays in literacy acquisition.

Motivation plays a powerful role in children's literacy growth and development. In fact, research shows that motivated students choose to read, read more, and become better readers than their less motivated peers (Guthrie & Wigfield, 2000; Malloy, Marinak, & Gambrell, 2010). The choices motivated readers make contribute to an ever widening gap between less proficient and more proficient readers, a phenomenon often referred to as the *Matthew Effect* (Stanovich, 1986). In an effort to close this gap, attention to motivating children to read is perhaps as important as the instruction they receive.

This study explores the role of motivation in the literacy development of struggling readers in first grade. The participants in the study were 1,334 children who received the Reading Recovery intervention in the fall of first grade, and a comparison group of 472 children who were similar in reading proficiency but did not receive the Reading Recovery intervention. Reading Recovery is a short-term early intervention for first-grade students who have the lowest achievement on measures of literacy outcomes. In the Reading Recovery intervention, students meet individually with a specially trained teacher for 30 min each day for a period of 12–20 weeks. The goal during this period is for children to develop a network of reading and writing strategies so they may independently perform within the average range of their peers.

Reading Recovery uses the *Observation Survey of Early Literacy Achievement* (OSELA; Clay, 2013) as a screening and instructional tool. OSELA adheres to accepted standards of assessment, including attention to content and construct validity and reliability (Denton, Ciancio, & Fletcher, 2006) and uses six subtasks to measure letter identification, word reading, phonemic awareness, writing vocabulary, concepts of print, and text reading level. The assessment does not include a measure of children's motivation to read.

In most schools in the United States, first grade is the period when students begin the journey of learning to read. Motivation to read, however, begins to develop well before first grade (Saracho & Dayton, 1991). In a study examining children's perceptions about reading, Lever-Chain (2008) found that male pre-K students already have ideas about what it means to be a proficient reader and that, by the end of kindergarten, they may develop perceptions about the difficulty of reading. As students transition into first grade, instructional factors also begin to influence reading proficiency and motivation (Foorman, Francis, Fletcher, Schatschneider, & Mehta, 1998). First grade becomes a pivotal time not only for students' reading acquisition, but for the ways in which motivation contributes to reading development. Because reading proficiency and motivation appear to be inextricably linked, it is important to provide early intervention for a child that jointly addresses both constructs. Therefore, the primary purpose of this investigation was to test the hypothesis that an instructional intervention based on principles of motivation is likely to support both reading achievement and motivation to read.

Theoretical frameworks

This study draws on a number of theoretical frameworks for reading motivation including expectancy-value theory (Wigfield & Eccles, 2000), engagement theory (Guthrie & Wigfield, 2000), and sociocultural theory (Vygotsky, 1978). The expectancy-value theory of motivation posits that motivation is influenced by the students' perceptions, whether they perceive that they will be successful in performing the reading task (expectancy) and whether they perceive the reading task to be relevant and important (value). A central goal of reading instruction is to support and nurture the development of reading engagement. Guthrie and Wigfield's engagement theory is based on the premise that motivation to read is a precursor for reading engagement (Bogner, Raphael, & Pressley, 2002). Moreover, students who are inherently interested, or intrinsically motivated, choose to read (Ryan & Deci, 2000). Guthrie (2004) found that intrinsically motivated students also spend more time reading and are more engaged while reading. As students engage in literacy tasks, their reading abilities are more likely to improve. With this success, children are further motivated to engage with text as they read and extend their knowledge (Guthrie, 1999).

According to Morgan and Fuchs (2007), given sufficient print resources (Neuman & Celano, 2001), there are two factors that explain how often a child chooses to read. The first factor is initial success in developing reading skills and the second is motivation (Cunningham & Stanovich, 1997). Guthrie (1999) concluded that motivation is the preeminent predictor of students' frequent engagement in reading. Thus, poor readers' lack of motivation to read is thought to be an underlying cause of reading difficulties. Morgan and Fuchs (2007) contend that understanding why struggling readers are poorly motivated may have implications for early intervention. They suggest the importance of understanding how poor reading skills and low motivation interrelate when addressing these aspects of reading development.

In a review of the research on the relationship between students' reading proficiency and reading motivation, the results supported the conclusion that reading skill correlates with reading motivation (Morgan & Fuchs, 2007). In addition, the results tentatively supported the hypothesis that reading achievement and reading motivation predict each other over time. Morgan and Fuchs's findings offer support for the notion of a bidirectional relationship between reading proficiency and reading motivation. Thus, reading skills and motivation appear to influence each other, indicating interventions for struggling readers should target both aspects.

The principles of Reading Recovery and the instruction students receive focuses on increasing reading skills and reading motivation. Because Reading Recovery teachers recognize motivational factors as a crucial part of a student's reading journey, the social context in which instruction takes place is always considered. This includes the ways in which teacher–student interactions take shape in a socially constructed environment (Fullerton & Forbes, 2014). *Sociocultural theory* states that a child's cognitive development must be viewed individually and socially (Vygotsky, 1978). A major tenet of sociocultural theory, the zone of proximal development, has been addressed in Reading Recovery through the use of *scaffolding* (Wood, Bruner, & Ross, 1976). Scaffolding involves providing support for a child's thinking through teacher prompting and questioning. As a result of this support, the child internalizes the experience on the intrapsychological plane and later uses this to solve problems independently.

Review of related research on motivation and Reading Recovery

This review of the research focuses on two areas of interest related to the current study. First, our review examines the research conducted on young children's motivation to read. Second, we review research on reading motivation that has been conducted with students who have participated in Reading Recovery.

Research on dimensions of motivation

Much focus has been given to dimensions of motivation including intrinsic and extrinsic motivation, motivational goals, self-efficacy, and social motivation (Gambrell & Morrow, 1996; Wigfield & Guthrie, 1997). For this article, motivational studies conducted in the last 15 years were reviewed to examine how the instructional components of motivation were represented in the literature on early reading. The review yielded four components: interest, challenge, collaboration, and self-efficacy.

Interest. Student interest has been shown to positively affect student engagement (Bogner et al., 2002). Capturing interest can be accomplished in a variety of ways, including matching books to students' curiosities as a means of motivating and engaging students. Furthermore, Nolen (2007) found that books by the same author helped students develop an ongoing interest in certain genres. In addition to developing these types of interests, students can also form an interest in the act of reading. Joint storybook reading that yields affective reading interactions can contribute to student interest (Sonnenschein & Munsterman, 2002) if the interactions are enjoyable and rich in conversational interchange (Guthrie, 1999). Creating a pleasant context and using appealing text builds interest that furthers motivation to read.

Reading Recovery teachers focus on establishing a relationship with the child to build on the student's interests (Lyons, 2003). Through conversations during the reading and writing components of the lesson, teachers learn about students' interests, likes, and dislikes (DeFord, 1994). Teachers carefully select texts, which not only support the child's literacy processing system, but also build upon his or her interests. Additionally, at times during the lesson, students have the opportunity to select books they find appealing.

Challenge. When students are motivated, they are drawn to challenges (Gambrell & Morrow, 1996). Bogner and colleagues (2002) found when teachers supported risk-taking while providing and encouraging challenging opportunities, students' motivation increased. Challenge can also be moderated by a teacher's ability to scaffold students' performance (Wood et al., 1976). Scaffolding is the way in which a teacher demonstrates, guides, and adjusts the level of challenge to meet students' needs (Rodgers, 2004). Creating the appropriate level of challenge during scaffolding keeps the learner engaged without frustrating them (Powell, McIntyre, & Rightmyer, 2006). Scaffolding should account for the student's strengths and should be lifted over time as students take on tasks independently. Scaffolded interactions are supported by the collaborative relationship between teacher and child (Lyons, 2003).

The ongoing assessment and close observation of children in Reading Recovery (Clay, 2001) provides teachers with formative information to plan lessons that support students in reading increasing challenging text. Observation affords the teacher with the opportunities to carefully note how a child responds to prompts or other scaffolded interactions. Close observation of the child, coupled with anecdotal records of the observation, allows the teacher to reflect on the interactions and modulate the support the child needs (Clay & Cazden, 1990). For example, a teacher may recognize that supportive comments may be needed to assist the child in constructing meaning, particularly as the child moves from one page to another. Such scaffolding provides additional support and assists in mediating the child's understanding of the text. As part of the assessment cycle, teachers note the child's response to the provided support, determine if it is beneficial, adjust the level of support if needed, and eventually lift the scaffold as the child gains independence (Rodgers, 2004).

Collaboration. Collaborations allow opportunities for students to further learning and increase motivation to read. Teachers play a large role in a child's motivation to read and their deliberate and conscious actions are necessary in order to motivate students. "Not all instructional tasks are equally motivating to young learners, nor are they equally empowering" (Powell et al., 2006, p. 24). According to Bogner and colleagues (2002), an overwhelming amount of positive motivation is needed to empower students, particularly struggling learners. In addition to a positive atmosphere, teacher–student collaborations are key to helping students grow as readers. During teacher–student collaborations, scaffolding becomes especially important to building positive changes in motivation and cognitive processes (Lyons, 2003).

Reading Recovery builds on the importance of teacher–student collaboration. Teacher–student collaboration in Reading Recovery is reflected in the way the teacher responds to and follows the lead of the student. This is sometimes viewed as a collaborative dance. This collaboration takes place during the lesson and is reflected in the scaffolded interactions between the teacher and child. It is also evident following the lesson as the teacher continues to follow the lead of the child to plan subsequent instruction. This process allows the teacher to build on what the child knows instead of relying on scripted instruction (Clay, 2001).

Self-efficacy. Research indicates a strong correlation between self-efficacy and perceived competence for literacy tasks (Wilson & Trainin, 2007). Although highly correlated, self-efficacy and competence are separate constructs. Students with higher literacy achievement credit internal aspects like effort, while lower achievers credit external factors (Bogner et al., 2002). High achievers believe their abilities change with effort and teachers who encourage this changeable intelligence help develop self-efficacy in their students (Dweck, 2006).

The gradual release of responsibility allows students' ownership of their reading and supports independence and self-efficacy (Lyons, 2003). Because Reading Recovery teachers are trained to closely observe children, they are continually aware of how students are responding to instruction. As a result, once children have demonstrated control of a particular reading behavior, the scaffold is lifted, thus increasing feelings of independence and self-efficacy.

Research on motivation in Reading Recovery

Increasing students' motivation to read is a key principle of Reading Recovery instruction and a number of studies have investigated the reading motivation of students who have participated in the Reading Recovery intervention (Cohen, McDonnell, & Osborn, 1989; Fullerton & Forbes, 2014; Townsend, Townsend, & Seo, 2001; Wade & Moore, 1998). Cohen and colleagues (1989) compared students in Reading Recovery to higher achieving students using an attribution scale and a self-efficacy scale. At posttest, the two groups' average motivation levels did not differ significantly, suggesting the Reading Recovery students became more like the higher achieving students (yet the results were inconclusive because pretest group differences were only assumed by the authors rather than being factored into their statistical analyses).

A study by Wade and Moore (1998) examined the reading motivation of students 5 years after completing the Reading Recovery intervention. They compared the former Reading Recovery students in the same year with students who had average or below average reading skills. Although the comparison group had higher reading ability in the first year, 5 years later the former Reading Recovery students had better reading comprehension and were more positive about reading than the non-Reading Recovery students.

In a retrospective study, Townsend and colleagues (2001) explored the motivational effects of Reading Recovery on self-concept and task value. One group of students received Reading Recovery, a second group consisted of students who were eligible for Reading Recovery but did not receive the intervention, and a third group consisted of participants who did not qualify for Reading Recovery. Motivation was assessed using the Motivation to Read Profile (MRP; Gambrell, Palmer, Codling, & Mazzoni, 1996) and comprehension assessments. Overall findings revealed that mean reading scores were higher for Reading Recovery students than the non-Reading Recovery group with a statistically significant difference on comprehension in favor of the Reading Recovery group. With respect to reading motivation, Reading Recovery children's responses were all in positive directions on the MRP but there were no statistically significant differences among the groups. Across all three of these studies, motivation was higher for Reading Recovery students following the intervention.

In a more recent study, Fullerton and Forbes (2014) investigated whether there was a change in students' motivational responses from entry to exit point in Reading Recovery using the Children's Reading Motivation Survey (Mazzoni, Gambrell, & Korkeamaki, 1999). This study documented a substantial increase in motivation from the time the students entered the Reading Recovery program to the end of the intervention. This finding held for both girls and boys. Fullerton and Forbes concluded that after the intervention, "the Reading Recovery children's motivational responses were significantly more positive than prior to the intervention" (p. 49).

Though a number of studies have examined motivation and Reading Recovery, the inferences drawn from the studies are tenuous due to methodological limitations. The major drawback of the reviewed studies was the lack of a proper counterfactual because the studies relied on pretest-posttest motivation gains alone, or a nonequivalent comparison group without pretest adjustments. Fullerton and Forbes (2014) suggested that future research should include a comparison group not receiving the intervention so causal connections could be explored.

In this study, as suggested by Fullerton and Forbes (2014), we compared the pre- and post- achievement and motivation levels of Reading Recovery students to a comparison group of the next lowest band students, which allowed us to better isolate the role of motivation in Reading Recovery. We examined the effects of Reading Recovery on student achievement and motivation, and the degree to which each variable potentially mediated the effect of Reading Recovery on the other variable. Using structural equation modeling, we first examined the direct effect of the Reading Recovery intervention on students' posttest achievement and motivation levels after controlling for their initial levels of achievement and motivation. We hypothesized that Reading Recovery would have significant and positive effects on both variables with covariate adjustments. Yet because Reading Recovery is designed to primarily affect achievement, we assumed the treatment effect would be stronger for achievement than for motivation.

After addressing direct treatment effects, we examined the mediating roles of both motivation and achievement within the latticework of effects. Treating posttest achievement as the outcome, we expected that the intervention would have a direct positive effect on student's motivation levels, and that increased motivation levels would in turn affect students' achievement levels. Thus, we expected to find that Reading Recovery would improve students' motivation and achievement directly, but additionally, that improvements in motivation would also lead to increased levels of achievement. Due to the bidirectional nature of motivation and achievement, we also assumed that Reading Recovery would have a significant and positive effect on motivation, with achievement mediating the relationship. We particularly focused on which pattern of effects (motivation mediating achievement or achievement mediating motivation) fit the data best.

Method

Participants

Data from 1,806 students in 225 schools throughout South Carolina were used for the analysis in this study. Students in Reading Recovery ($n = 1,334$) during the first part of the 2012–2013 school year served as the treatment group. In each participating school, Reading Recovery teachers were asked to identify between four to ten students in the next achievement tier who potentially were eligible or were near eligible for Reading Recovery but who did not receive the intervention. Those students served as the comparison group ($n = 472$), and represented a subgroup of children who were slightly more proficient than Reading Recovery students at the beginning of the school year, and thus, were the closest students (achievement-wise) at each school to the treatment children. The demographic profiles of the two student groups reflected this comparability with slightly greater proportions of conventionally used indicators of need. The percentage of boys in the treatment group was 61% compared to 56% among comparison students, and 53% of treatment students and 55% of comparison students were ethnic minorities. The groups also were comparable in terms of free or reduced-price lunch eligibility, with 70% and 72% of treatment and comparison students qualifying, respectively. Nine percent of comparison students were English Language Learners (ELL), whereas 12% of treatment students were classified as ELL.

Measures

There were two primary measures used in this study, the Me and My Reading Profile (MMRP; Marinak, Malloy, Gambrell, & Mazzoni, 2015), and the Observation Survey of Early Literacy Achievement (OSELA; Clay, 2013). Reading Recovery and comparison children were administered both measures in the fall before the intervention (Time 1) and midyear after the treatment period (Time 2).

Based on the expectancy-value theory (Wigfield & Eccles, 2000), the MMRP consists of 20 affective questions about reading that children answer using a three-option response scale. The MMRP was designed for children in Grades 1–3. To determine validity, exploratory factor analysis (using a varimax orthogonal rotation) was used to examine the interfactor correlations. Factor analysis revealed that the 20 items contributed to the two subscales of self-concept and value of reading in keeping with value-expectancy theory. However, a third factor (Literacy Out Loud) was identified related to interactions about literacy such as listening, speaking, and reading aloud to others. This factor reflects the social aspects of literacy commonly seen and heard in primary classrooms. Reliability analyses (Cronbach, 1951) revealed scale alphas ranging from .86 (self-concept) to .87 (value and Literacy Out Loud) with all items contributing to the over-all scale reliability.

Because reliability and validity for the MMRP (2015) was established based on students in Grades 1–3, the sample reflected a broad range of reading-proficiency levels. The present study focused on first-grade struggling readers, so we conducted an internal structural analysis based on the MMRP data in fall or midyear (Table 1). Table 1 presents the results of the internal structural analysis based on the data in fall and midyear. The items are ordered from the least fitting to most fitting items. There are absolute threshold values on the three indices that would indicate whether the item fit or did not fit a unidimensional scale, but common factor loadings below about .30, Rasch fit values above 2.00, and item-total point biserial correlations below about .25 indicate misfitting items. As can be seen, Items 2 and 20 have fit values that are near these commonly used thresholds, but the fit values for both items, and the remaining 18, reveal the MMRP questions appear to fit a unidimensional scale. The factorial structure also was maintained from pretest to posttest.

The alpha coefficients of the pretest and posttest data were .87, which also indicated that together the items create a single-dimension scale and yielded total MMRP values that were sufficiently reliable at both time points. As a final check on the unidimensionality of the MMRP both before and after treatment, we conducted a confirmatory factor analysis with latent variables at each time point. The covariance between the two latent variables was estimated freely. Weighted least square with mean- and variance-adjusted (WLSMV) estimation method provided by Mplus 7.2 was adopted with the assumption that the MMRP response scales were ordinal. Model fit indices were yielded as follows: χ^2 (739) = 3,272.786 ($p < .001$), RMSEA (Root Mean Square Error of Approximation) of 0.044 with a 90% confidence interval of (0.042, 0.045). CFI (comparative fit index) was .916, TLI (Tucker Lewis Index) was .911, suggesting that the measurement model fit the data reasonably well.

Table 1. Me and My Reading Profile (MMRP) dimensionality analysis of before and after treatment data ($n = 1,806$).

Item #s for the MMRP*	Before Treatment			After Treatment		
	Factor Loading	Rasch Misfit	Point Biserial	Factor Loading	Rasch Misfit	Point Biserial
2	.31	1.40	.30	.36	1.26	.29
20	.42	1.18	.39	.42	1.18	.32
5	.44	1.20	.48	.45	1.18	.48
9	.53	1.17	.55	.57	1.11	.58
7	.50	1.08	.50	.51	1.01	.50
8	.48	1.15	.49	.51	1.11	.49
1	.56	1.11	.52	.47	1.26	.45
6	.55	.96	.54	.52	.94	.56
19	.55	.99	.51	.50	1.01	.47
3	.57	.98	.53	.50	.99	.45
10	.55	1.02	.47	.53	1.10	.44
14	.54	1.05	.46	.59	1.00	.45
18	.54	.92	.49	.48	.94	.44
4	.56	.97	.51	.52	1.08	.47
16	.68	.92	.58	.62	1.03	.52
13	.64	.91	.58	.62	.92	.56
17	.65	.84	.57	.63	.86	.53
15	.66	.80	.57	.68	.79	.53
12	.67	.74	.60	.60	.78	.53
11	.73	.74	.61	.70	.77	.55

*See Marinak, Malloy, Gambrell, & Mazzoni (2015) for a description of the items on the MMRP.

The OSELA consists of six tasks, including Letter Identification, the Ohio Word Test, Concepts About Print, Writing Vocabulary, Text Reading Level, and Hearing and Recording Sounds in Words. Each of the six tasks alone has certain methodological limitations, such as floor effects or non-interval scales, so scores from the individual tasks were not used in this study. Instead, a total score based on Rasch measurement procedures was used to represent students' beginning and after-treatment literacy achievement (see D'Agostino, 2012, for the psychometric properties of the OSELA total score).

Analytic procedures

In order to test our hypotheses, we conducted structural equation modeling (SEM) using Mplus 7.2. SEM was suitable for our analytic purposes because it allows one to examine both direct effects and the role of mediating factors. Three primary models were fit to the data, one per research hypothesis. The three models are depicted in Figure 1. The first model examined the direct effect of Reading Recovery on posttest OSELA total scores and posttest MMRP scores while controlling for baseline OSELA achievement and MMRP motivation. The second model tested the direct effect of the intervention on achievement and the mediating effect of motivation, and the third model considered the direct treatment effect on motivation with a mediating effect of achievement.

The treatment and achievement variables are represented in the diagrams as rectangles because they are observed variables. Treatment was coded "*1*" for Reading Recovery students and "*0*" for comparison students. The achievement variables are students' OSELA total scores before (A1) and after (A2) the treatment. Pretest and posttest motivation (M1 & M2) are depicted with ellipses in the diagrams indicating that each was treated as a latent variable and measured with the twenty MMRP items at each of the two test time points. For all SEM models tested in this study, cut-off criteria for model fit indices were based on strategies suggested by Hu and Bentler (1999), giving: > .90 for comparative fit index (CFI) and Tucker-Lewis indices (TLI), and ≤ .08 for the root mean square error of approximation (RMSEA).

Model 1

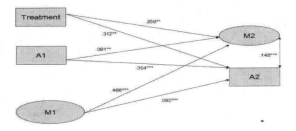

Model 2

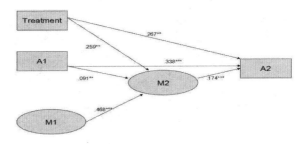

Model 3

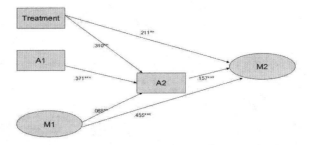

Figure 1. Final Tested Models in the study. Model 1 tests the direct effects of Reading Recovery on posttest achievement (A2) and motivation (M2) while controlling for pretest achievement (A1) and pretest motivation (M1). Model 2 tests the direct effect of Reading Recovery on A2 and the mediating effect of M2 while controlling for A1 and M1. Model 3 tests the direct Reading Recovery effect on M2 and the mediating effect of A2 while controlling for A1 and M1. *Note.* $^*p<.05.$ $^{**}p<.01.$ $^{***}p<.001.$

Results

Before testing the three SEM models, we examined the means and standard deviations of the key variables, as well as the correlations between the treatment variable (coded "*1*" for students who received Reading Recovery) and achievement and motivation at pretest and posttest. In order to provide the descriptive statistics for motivation at pretest and posttest, we computed the average raw score for each student across the 20 items at each time point. Reading Recovery students had a slightly lower motivation average at pretest (M = 2.37, SD = 0.43) than comparison students (M = 2.42, SD = 0.42), but at posttest, the treatment students had a larger average motivation score (M = 2.61, SD = 0.35) than their counterparts (M = 2.52, SD = 0.37). The same pretest to posttest differences were found for achievement. Reading Recovery students, on average had a 371 OSELA scale score (SD = 35.20), whereas the comparison students, on average had a

392 (SD = 33.93) scale score at the first time point. At posttest, the treatment students (M = 488, SD = 43.24) had a larger average scale score than the comparison students (M = 485, SD = 33.78). Besides the fact that students were not assigned randomly to receive Reading Recovery, the nonequivalent pretest means confirmed the need to control for initial group differences.

Table 2 provides the correlations among the variables. As can be seen from the table, Treatment was negatively related with pretest achievement (A1), and to a lesser extent pretest motivation (M1), which was expected given the pretest mean differences between the two groups. At posttest, treatment students had higher motivation scores and comparable achievement levels, on average, than comparison students as revealed by the positive correlation with posttest motivation (M2) and the non-significant association with posttest achievement (A2). Motivation and achievement were modestly correlated at baseline (0.11) and at posttest (.20), yet the two strongest correlations were between the two sets of variables over time; A1 and A2 (.33) and M1 and M2 (.48) with motivation having slightly greater consistency over time. This may say less about the consistency of the constructs and more about the primary purpose of the treatment, which is to spoil the prediction of later achievement.

Structural equation model findings

Table 3 presents the fit statistics for the three tested SEM models, and Figure 1 displays the path coefficients for the final tested models. We first examined the fit of Model 1, which tested the direct treatment effect on the two outcomes while controlling for baseline levels. The model fit the data reasonably well, as indicated by the fit statistic values. The root mean square error of approximation (RMSEA) was less than .08, and the comparative fit index (CFI) and Tucker-Lewis Index (TLI) both were greater than .90. As displayed in the table, the predictors explained a greater proportion of motivation at Time 2 variance (.23) than posttest achievement variance (.13), but the magnitude of the coefficients presented in the figure indicate that Reading Recovery participation was about equally associated with achievement ($B = .31$, $p < .001$) and motivation ($B = .26$, $p < .001$) at Time 2. Note that M1 explained more M2 variance than A1 explained A2 variance, perhaps leading to more total M2 variance explained than A2. Because the coefficients are interpretable as standardized beta coefficients, the values can be converted into standardized mean difference d values. The effect size of the intervention on achievement and motivation, respectively, was .65 and .54.

The sufficient fit of Model 1 indicated that Reading Recovery had a direct effect on both outcomes, but did not address if one outcome mediated the effect of the other outcome. To address that general question, we fit Models 2 and 3 to the data. After fitting Model 2 as depicted in Figure 1, the path from M1 to A2 was not significant ($p > .05$) so we decided to delete that particular path and recompute the model. The final model with coefficients is presented in Figure 2. As reflected by the fit statistic values (Table 3), Model 2 fit the data reasonably well, with fit values that were comparable to Model 1. The path coefficients reveal that A1 significantly and positively predicted M2 ($B = .09$, $p < .01$) as well as A2 ($B = .34$, $p < .001$), indicating that baseline achievement levels had significant positive effects on both motivation and achievement at Time 2. M1 significantly and positively predicted M2 ($B = .47$, $p < .001$), and M2, in turn, significantly predicted A2 ($B = .17$, $p < .001$), indicating that baseline motivation seemed to exert an effect on achievement indirectly through motivation at posttest. Reading Recovery significantly and positively predicted M2 ($B = .26$, $p < .01$) as well as A2 ($B = .27$, $p < .01$).

Table 2. Correlation matrix between key variables.

	Treatment	A1	A2	M1	M2
Treatment	1				
A1	−0.22***	1			
A2	0.03	0.33***	1		
M1	−0.06*	0.11***	0.12***	1	
M2	0.11***	0.07*	0.20***	.48***	1

Note. *$p < .05$. ***$p < .001$. Treatment coded 0 for comparison, 1 for Reading Recovery. Pretest Achievement (A1), posttest Achievement (A2), pretest Motivation (M1), posttest Motivation (M2).

Table 3. Fit statistics for the three models.

	Model		
	1	2	3
χ^2	3,052.9*(855)	3,035.5*(856)	3,026.4*(856)
RMSEA	.041(.040 − .043)	.041(.039 − .043)	.041(.039 − .043)
CFI	.916	.917	.917
TLI	.911	.912	.913

Note. RMSEA = Root Mean Square Error of Approximation; CFI = Comparative Fit Index; TLI = Tucker-Lewis Index.

Because M2 predicted A2, the model reveals that M2 apparently mediated the treatment effect on achievement to some extent. Recall from Model 1 that the standardized coefficient indexing the treatment effect on achievement was .312 after controlling for pretest achievement and motivation and without considering the mediating effect of posttest motivation. The inclusion of the mediating motivation variable reduced the direct effect size estimate to .267. The remaining .045 treatment effect can be found in the indirect effect through M2, which also can be computed by multiplying the treatment to M2 coefficient (.259) by the M2 to A2 coefficient (.174). Thus, the mediating effect of motivation accounts for about 14% of the Reading Recovery effect on posttest achievement (.045/.312).

We also fit Model 3 to the data, which allowed us to examine the degree to which achievement mediated the Reading Recovery effect on motivation. As can be seen from Table 3, the fit statistic values for Model 3 were comparable to the values for Models 1 and 2. In terms of the role achievement plays in mediating the treatment effect on motivation, consider from Model 1 that the direct treatment effect coefficient was .267. From Figure 2, it can be seen that, with A2 mediating the relationship, the direct effect coefficient for the intervention on M2 was reduced to .211. The indirect effect through A2 was .049 (.310 times .157). Therefore, the indirect effect through A2 accounted for about 18% of the overall treatment effect on motivation (.049/.267).

Discussion

The primary goal of this study was to investigate the role that motivation may play in accounting for the effect of an early literacy intervention, Reading Recovery, on students' achievement levels. Using a quasi-experimental design and SEM as the statistical analytic tool, we estimated the Reading Recovery effect size to be .65 on achievement and .54 on motivation after controlling for baseline achievement and motivational differences between the Reading Recovery treatment group and comparison group.

We also found that motivation mediated the treatment effect on achievement, and achievement mediated the effect on motivation. In the former mediation model, the indirect effect through motivation explained about 14% of achievement effect, and in the latter model, the indirect effect through achievement explained about 18% of the motivation effect. All three models, whether the direct effects model or mediation models, fit the data equally well. Thus, it was not possible to conclude that one model was superior to the other two in terms of explaining the interplay between motivation and achievement in Reading Recovery. It was possible, based on the SEM results, to support a direct effects model, or one of the two mediation models. There appears to be a bidirectional process by which motivational and achievement changes affect one another in a symbiotic manner, and although Reading Recovery is designed specifically to address children's actual reading processes, it is not possible to ignore the role motivation plays in learning how to read.

Although we set out to examine the role of motivation in Reading Recovery by employing a more rigorous methodological design than found in prior studies, our investigation had limitations. We detected at pretest that the treatment and control groups did not have equivalent achievement and motivation levels, on average, which indicated the need to control for initial group differences. Nonetheless, covariate analysis can over- or under-adjust initial differences, making causal inferences less tenable than more rigorous designs such as randomized trials. Besides the limitations with covariate analyses, the comparative results between motivation and achievement may have been influenced by restricted variability on the motivation measure at posttest, which could have led to underestimations of its role in the intervention effects. Future studies should address these issues in order to produce stronger inferences regarding Reading Recovery's effect on motivation, and the moderating role motivation may play in explaining achievement gains resulting from the intervention.

Reading Recovery teachers go through an intensive year of university-based training and continue to participate in ongoing embedded professional development in subsequent years. This initial and ongoing learning focuses not only on children's literacy processing, but also on the relationship between emotion and cognition including motivational dynamics. The earlier review of existing motivation literature revealed a number of influencing factors including interest, challenge, collaboration, and self-efficacy. These factors are accounted for in the intervention and could contribute to children in Reading Recovery having a more positive attitude toward reading than their like peers to whom they were compared in this study.

During lessons, Reading Recovery teachers engage students' attention and interest. When selecting new books for a student, teachers consider the opportunities that a text will offer, and carefully match the challenges to the strengths and needs of the child. During the new book selection, teachers also carefully consider the students' personal interests. Many of the books used in the intervention build on familiar characters that reappear across the text level gradient. As noted earlier, books in a series or books by the same author help students develop an ongoing interest in reading (Nolen, 2007). Eventually these books, which were once at the child's instructional level, are read independently. One component of the 30-min lesson involves the rereading of these now independent and familiar texts. The purpose of this portion of the lesson is to have children orchestrate the reading process in a prosodic and fluent manner, in turn bolstering self-efficacy through successful and autonomous engagement with text (Clay, 2001).

In addition to accounting for children's interests, Reading Recovery teachers also recognize the importance of enlisting children's strengths in teaching and learning (Clay, 1990). Identifying what the students know and building on the known are key components. Reading Recovery teachers are versed in keeping it easy to learn (Clay, 2001). This does not mean that children are not challenged. Instead, teachers are trained to provide support through scaffolded interactions with children (Wood et al., 1976). Teachers become close observers of children (Clay, 2001) and through the use of detailed records document the patterns of response between teacher and student in order to modulate the support they provide (Rodgers, 2004). Through this type of contingent instruction, teachers ensure the bar is constantly lifted by releasing more responsibility for the task to the child (Pearson & Gallagher, 1983). As a result of this fine-tuned support, children experience success and are more likely to stay engaged in the task of reading. Teachers' understanding of challenge and the ways in which they support problem-solving help confirm that instruction is within the students' zone of proximal development (Vygotsky, 1978). This reduces the likelihood of children experiencing the type of frustration that can lower motivation. When children are frustrated, they often avoid the task. Frustration is controlled through the collaborative relationship that develops between teacher and child. The relationship motivates the learner as the teacher and child jointly participate in the task (Rogoff, 1990).

Conclusion

Early reading interventions must consider the role motivation plays in literacy acquisition. If motivational factors are taken into account, children will be more successful in an intervention. Guthrie (1999) cautions "when the written code predominates children's consciousness of what it means to be a reader, a serious obstacle to intrinsically motivated reading arises" (p. 154). Reading is a complex process and attention to motivation must be an integral part of instruction. Approaching intervention from this perspective makes it more likely that children not only learn to read, but choose to read.

References

Bogner, K., Raphael, L., & Pressley, M. (2002). How grade 1 teachers motivate literate activity by their students. *Scientific Studies of Reading, 6*(2), 135–165. doi: 10.1207/s1532799xssr0602_02

Clay, M. M. (1990). Learning to be learning disabled. *New Zealand Journal of Educational Studies, 22*(2), 155–173.

Clay, M. M. (2001). *Change over time in children's literacy development*. Portsmouth, NH: Heinemann.

Clay, M. M. (2013). *An observation survey of early literacy achievement*. Portsmouth, NH: Heinemann.

Clay, M. M., & Cazden, C. B. (1990). A Vygotskian interpretation of Reading Recovery. In L. Moll (Ed.), *Vygotsky and education: Instructional implications and applications of sociohistorical psychology* (pp. 206–222). New York, NY: Cambridge University Press.

Cohen, S. G., McDonnell, G., & Osborn, B. (1989). Self-perceptions of at risk and high achieving readers: Beyond Reading Recovery achievement data. In S. McCormick & J. Zutell (Eds.), *Cognitive and social perspectives for literacy research and instruction: Thirty-eighth yearbook of the National Reading Conference* (pp. 117–122). Chicago, IL: National Reading Conference.

Cronbach, L. J. (1951). Coefficient alpha and the internal structure of tests. *Psychometrika, 16*(3), 297–334. doi: 10.1007/bf02310555

Cunningham, A. E., & Stanovich, K. E. (1997). Early reading acquisition and its relation to reading experience and ability 10 years later. *Developmental Psychology, 33*(6), 934–945. doi: 10.1037/0012-1649.33.6.934

D'Agostino, J. V. (2012). U.S. norm trends and recommendations on Observation Survey total score use. *Journal of Reading Recovery, 12*, 59–64.

DeFord, D. E. (1994). Early writing: Teachers and children in Reading Recovery. *Literacy, Teaching and Learning: An International Journal of Early Literacy, 1*, 31–56.

Denton, C. A., Ciancio, D. J., & Fletcher, J. M. (2006). Validity, reliability, and utility of the Observation Survey of Early Literacy Achievement. *Reading Research Quarterly, 41*, 8–34. doi: 10.1598/rrq.41.1.1

Dweck, C. (2006). *Mindset: The new psychology of success*. New York, NY: Random House.

Foorman, B. R., Francis, D. J., Fletcher, J. M., Schatschneider, C., & Mehta, P. (1998). The role of instruction in learning to read: Preventing reading failure in at-risk children. *Journal of Educational Psychology, 90*, 37–55. doi:10.1037/0022-0663.90.1.37

Fullerton, S. K., & Forbes, S. (2014). Motivational changes in Reading Recovery children: A pre and post analysis. *Journal of Reading Recovery, 13*, 43–53.

Gambrell, L. B., & Morrow, L. M. (1996). Creating motivating contexts for literacy learning. In L. Baker, P. Afflerbach, & D. Reinking (Eds.), *Developing engaged readers in school and home communities* (pp. 115–136). Mahwah, NJ: Erlbaum.

Gambrell, L. B., Palmer, B. M., Codling, R. M., & Mazzoni, S. A. (1996). Assessing motivation to read. *Reading Teacher, 49*(7), 518–533. doi:10.1598/rt.49.7.2

Guthrie, J. T. (1999). The young reader as a self-extending system: Motivational and cognitive underpinnings. In J. S. Gaffney & B. J. Askew (Eds.), *Stirring the waters: The influence of Marie Clay* (pp. 149–163). Portsmouth, NH: Heinemann.

Guthrie, J. T. (2004). Teaching for literacy engagement. *Journal of Literacy Research, 36*, 1–29. doi: 10.1207/s15548430jlr3601_2

Guthrie, J. T., & Wigfield, A. (2000). Engagement and motivation in reading. In M. L. Kamil, P. B. Mosenthal, P. D. Pearson, & R. Barr (Eds.), *Handbook of reading research: Vol. III* (pp. 403–422). New York, NY: Routledge.

Hu, L., & Bentler, P. M. (1999). Cutoff criteria for fit indexes in covariance structure analysis: Conventional criteria versus new alternatives. *Structural Equation Modeling: A Multidisciplinary Journal, 6*, 1–55. doi:10.1080/10705519909540118

Lever-Chain, J. (2008). Turning boys off? Listening to what five-year-olds say about reading. *Literacy, 42*, 83–91. doi:10.1111/j.1741-4369.2008.00488.x

Lyons, C. A. (2003). *Teaching struggling readers: How to use brain-based research to maximize learning*. Portsmouth, NH: Heinemann.

Malloy, J. A., Marinak, B. A., & Gambrell, L. B. (2010). *Essential readings on motivation*. Newark, DE: International Reading Association.

Marinak, B. A., Malloy, J. A., Gambrell, L. B., & Mazzoni, S. A. (2015). Me and my reading profile: A tool for assessing early reading motivation. *Reading Teacher, 69*(1), 51–62. doi: 10.1002/trtr.1362

Mazzoni, S. A., Gambrell, L. B., & Korkeamaki, R. L. (1999). A cross-cultural perspective of early literacy motivation. *Journal of Reading Psychology, 20*(3), 237–253. doi:10.1080/027027199278411

Morgan, P. L., & Fuchs, D. (2007). Is there a bidirectional relationship between children's reading skills and reading motivation? *Exceptional Children, 73*, 165–183. doi: 10.1177/001440290707300203

Neuman, S. B., & Celano, D. (2001). Access to print in low-income and middle-income communities: An ecological study of four neighborhoods. *Reading Research Quarterly, 36*(1), 8–26. doi:10.1598/rrq.36.1.1

Nolen, S. B. (2007). Construction literacy in the kindergarten: Task structure, collaboration, and motivation. *Cognition and Instruction, 19*, 95–142. doi: 10.1207/s1532690xci1901_3

Pearson, P. D., & Gallagher, M. (1983). The instruction of reading comprehension. *Contemporary Educational Psychology, 8*(3), 217–344. doi: 10.1016/0361-476x(83)90019-x

Powell, R., McIntyre, E., & Rightmyer, E. (2006). Johnny won't read, and Susie won't either: Reading instruction and student resistance. *Journal of Early Childhood Literacy, 6*, 5–31. doi: 10.1177/1468798406062172

Rodgers, E. M. (2004). Interactions that scaffold reading performance. *Journal of Literacy Research, 36*(4), 501–532. doi: 10.1207/s15548430jlr3604_4

Rogoff, B. (1990). *Apprenticeship in thinking: Cognitive development in social context.* New York, NY: Oxford University Press.

Ryan, R. M., & Deci, E. L. (2000). Intrinsic and extrinsic motivations: Classic definitions and new directions. *Contemporary Educational Psychology, 25*, 54–67. doi:10.1006/ceps.1999.1020

Saracho, O. N., & Dayton, C. M. (1991). Age-related changes in reading attitudes of young children: A cross-cultural study. *Journal of Research in Reading, 14*, 33–45. doi:10.1111/j.1467-9817.1991.tb00004.x

Sonnenschein, S., & Munsterman, K. (2002). The influence of home-based reading interactions on 5-year-olds' reading motivations and early literacy development. *Early Childhood Research Quarterly, 17*(3), 318–337. doi: 10.1016/s0885-2006(02)00167-9

Stanovich, K. E. (1986). Matthew effects in reading: Some consequences of individual differences in the acquisition of literacy. *Reading Research Quarterly, 21*(4), 360–406.

Townsend, M. A. R., Townsend, J. E., & Seo, K. J. (2001). Children's motivation to read following Reading Recovery. In J. V. Hoffman, D. L. Schallert, C. M. Fairbanks, J. Worthy, & B. Maloch (Eds.), *Fiftieth yearbook of the National Reading Conference* (pp. 584–596). Chicago, IL: National Reading Conference.

Vygotsky, L. S. (1978). *Mind and society: The development of higher mental processes.* Cambridge, MA: Harvard University Press.

Wade, B., & Moore, M. (1998). An early start with books: Literacy and mathematical evidence from a longitudinal study. *Educational Review, 50*(2), 135–145. doi: 10.1080/0013191980500205

Wigfield, A., & Eccles, J. S. (2000). Expectancy-value theory of achievement motivation. *Contemporary Educational Psychology, 25*, 68–81. doi: 10.1006/ceps.1999.1015

Wigfield, A., & Guthrie, J. T. (1997). Relations of children's motivation for reading to the amount and breadth of their reading. *Journal of Educational Psychology, 89*(3), 420–432. doi: 10.1037/0022-0663.89.3.420

Wilson, K. M., & Trainin, G. (2007). First-grade students' motivation and achievement for reading, writing, and spelling. *Reading Psychology, 28*(3), 257–282. doi: 10.1080/02702710601186464

Wood, D., Bruner, J. S., & Ross, G. (1976). The role of tutoring in problem solving. *Journal of Child Psychology and Psychiatry, 17*, 89–100. doi: 10.1111/j.1469-7610.1976.tb00381.x

Getting to Scale: Evidence, Professionalism, and Community

Robert E. Slavin

> **ABSTRACT**
> Evidence-based reform, in which proven programs are scaled up to reach many students, is playing an increasing role in American education. This article summarizes articles in this issue to explain how Reading Recovery has managed to sustain itself and go to scale over more than 30 years. It argues that Reading Recovery has succeeded due to a focus on *evidence*, *professionalism*, and *community*. Implications of the experience of Reading Recovery for policy and practice are discussed.

For a very long time, education policy in the United States has been driven by national, state, and local rules, funding schemes, and, since the early 1980s, test-based accountability. These policies may be necessary to ensure basic standards of education, but it is difficult to argue that they move systemwide outcomes forward. In reading, for example, national achievement in 2013 is only somewhat higher than it was in 1980 at all grade levels tested, and achievement gaps according to ethnicity and income have only diminished slightly (National Center for Education Statistics, 2015).

Alongside large-scale educational policies, there has existed a far smaller, but now growing, strategy for change: evidence-based reform. The idea behind evidence-based reform is to create replicable programs, test them in rigorous experiments, and then scale up those found to be effective to serve large numbers of students. Scaling up proven strategies has the advantage of starting with programs known to be effective, at least on a modest scale, in contrast to top-down strategies that affect much larger numbers of students right away but typically have unknown impacts until many years later, if ever.

The difficulty with the evidence-based reform strategy, however, is scale-up. How can proven programs grow to affect meaningful numbers of students without losing the qualities that made them effective in the first place?

Pitfalls of scale-up

To academics, the idea of establishing and evaluating programs and then scaling them up seems simple and straightforward. Doesn't everyone want better outcomes for children? Why wouldn't educators and policymakers enthusiastically adopt any approach proven to increase achievement?

The reality is quite different, however. First, most programs are not found to be effective in rigorous experiments. Even when programs do meet high standards of evidence, their developers may not be interested in scaling them up beyond their local area, if at all. If they do wish to take a program to scale, they may not have the financial resources or business skill to create an organization to support effective dissemination of a proven program. Even if they do have such capacity, they may not be able to ensure high-quality implementation at scale, so the initially effective approach may lose its effectiveness. National, state, and local policies and politics may turn against the program or deprive schools or program developers of resources to maintain dissemination, and these policies may create competing priorities for schools. Departure or retirement of program leaders may lead to difficulties in continuing dissemination. In light of these dangers and many more, it is remarkable when any program continues to scale up a proven program for many years.

The case of Reading Recovery

One of the very, very few unquestioned success stories of evidence-based reform is Reading Recovery (RR), the topic of the articles in this special issue. Originally created by Marie Clay in New Zealand, Reading Recovery was introduced in the United States in 1984 by researchers at Ohio State University, led by Gay Su Pinnell. RR is now disseminated by 19 universities throughout the United States, involving about 6,000 teachers and 47,000 students in 42 states (Rodgers, 2016).

The articles in this special issue tell the story of the extraordinary journey RR has undertaken over its 30-year history. Most importantly, they explain how RR managed to establish itself, build a strong research base, grow to serve large numbers of struggling readers, respond to major threats and policy shifts, and end up with a bright future.

Evidence, professionalism, and community

How did RR get to scale, maintain its effectiveness, and survive constant threats to its survival over so long a period? I put forward three key factors that explain their success: *evidence*, *professionalism*, and *community*.

Evidence means clear, replicated evidence from rigorous evaluations that show positive effects on children. Academics tend to assume that evidence is, of course, essential to scale-up in education, despite constant observations that evidence is not required for commercial products or programs, politically mandated practices, or practices adopted and maintained due to their correspondence with widely held ideologies among educators themselves. Yet to take to scale a specific program that is not supported by commercial interests, politics, or ideology, evidence is in fact essential. Or to put it another way, evidence is no match for marketing, mandates, or faddism, but it provides the only entry point for academics and other outsiders to affect the education of significant numbers of children.

The article by D'Agostino and Harmey (2016) summarizes research on RR, and uses the evidence to respond to longstanding criticisms of the program. In a one-to-one tutoring program administered by extensively trained teachers (rather than paraprofessionals) it would be astonishing if outcomes were not positive, so much of the review focuses appropriately on how positive they are. The article and another by Bates, D'Agostino, Gambrell, and Xu (2016), discuss moderators, sustained effects, and other issues of importance. However, the most crucial findings are those that have been established and uncontested since the 1980s. RR works. What this means is that in schools throughout the United States and in other countries, there is a well-defined group of struggling readers that can readily be taught to read. This evidence establishes, beyond any doubt, that nothing about these children means they are doomed to fail in reading. Could other approaches be equally effective or more cost-effective? It's, of course, possible. Might students who succeed in RR still need additional boosters of one kind or another beyond first grade? Perhaps. Are there children who do not benefit from RR? Of course, but as RR leaders have always said, failure in RR is the best diagnostic indicator known for out-of-the-ordinary reading difficulties.

Knowledge that the reading skills of most struggling readers can be substantially improved should be of enormous policy importance. There are about 4,000,000 first graders in the United States at any given time. Assume that 20% or 800,000 have moderate to severe reading difficulties. Yet RR serves only 47,000 students, or 6%. Imagine that other proven tutoring models collectively serve another 6%. Whatever the exact numbers, it is clear that this crucial problem, which RR has shown to be solvable in studies over 30 years, is still not being solved in the great majority of schools.

Professionalism

To scale up a proven program, evidence is not enough. Far from it. The program must be made explicit and replicable, with well-defined procedures for professional development, materials assessments, and other supports.

In many ways, these explicit supports and procedures run against the grain of American education, which generally prefers to try to manipulate teachers with standards and assessments but then to leave them alone to figure out how to achieve those standards. However, explicit procedures, implemented with intelligence and adaptability by well-trained interventionists, is the very essence of professionalism.

A professional is someone who has received extensive training to apply highly specialized approaches to complex problems. Professionals adapt to each particular problem, but they do not make it up as they go along. Imagine, for example, that surgeons were held accountable for their success rates, but given little guidance or support in evidence-based techniques for carrying out various surgeries.

From the outset, RR has provided extraordinary training to its teachers and teacher leaders. Using behind-the-glass observations, teachers are observed working with children, and are given detailed feedback and support over an extended period (see Rodgers, 2016). A RR teacher possesses unique and powerful skills. I know of no successful educational intervention that does not provide extensive professional development in well-specified procedures, and seeks to create both a spirit and an actuality of professionalism. Effective programs leave as little as possible to chance.

The focus on professionalism is not only essential for effectiveness. It is also essential for sustainability. Teachers and other educators who know they are professionals will fight for their profession. They have seen what they can accomplish and do not lightly abandon an effective approach.

Community

To go beyond a few local schools, developers of proven programs must develop regional or national organizations to carry forward the work. Rodgers (2016) describes how RR works primarily through partnerships with other universities. However, an effective scale-up organization is not just the people who provide the service, it's everyone involved—faculty members, teachers, leaders, everyone. Peurach and Glazer (2016) discuss this aspect of RR in detail. They describe the RR community as an "epistemic community," which is an overly academic way of saying that all members of the community are engaged in a process of learning and contributing intellectually to a whole that is bigger than themselves. This sense of community is intentionally built in RR and in other organizations going to scale. It is enhanced by a focus on professionalism, and like professionalism, community contributes both to effectiveness and to sustainability. Members of a high-status community of professionals will fight to maintain their community and will work to bring in and orient new members.

Conclusion

As the articles in this issue attest, RR presents a unique challenge to American education. It has shown again and again that it works and that it can continue to work at any scale. In a country as wealthy as the United States, why should every struggling reader not have access to RR or a tutoring program with equal evidence of effectiveness? The reading success of first graders is far too important to leave to chance, yet in this as in many other areas of education reform, vulnerable children are left to chance every day. Why can't educators use what they know to solve the problems they can solve, while working at the same time to expand their knowledge?

References

Bates, C. C., D'Agostino, J. V., Gambrell, L., & Xu, M. (2016). Reading Recovery: Exploring the effects on first graders' reading motivation and achievement. *Journal of Education for Students Placed At Risk, 21*, 47–59.

D'Agostino, J. V., & Harmey, S. J. (2016). An international meta-analysis of Reading Recovery. *Journal of Education for Students Placed At Risk, 21*, 29–46.

National Center for Education Statistics. (2015). *National Assessment of Educational Progress: Reading, 2013*. Available at http://nationsreportcard/reading/

Peurach, D. J., & Glazer, J. L. (2016). Introduction: Reading Recovery as an epistemic community. *Journal of Education for Students Placed At Risk, 21*, 1–9.

Rodgers, E. (2016). Scaling and sustaining an intervention: The case of Reading Recovery. *Journal of Education for Students Placed At Risk, 21*, 10–28.

Examining the Sustained Effects of Reading Recovery

Jerome V. D'Agostino, Mary K. Lose, and Robert H. Kelly

> **ABSTRACT**
> Though the immediate effect of Reading Recovery (RR) is both strong and well established, the longer term or sustained effect has been less studied and the evidence regarding it has been less conclusive. Michigan Reading Recovery students ($n = 328$) were compared to control students ($n = 264$) while in first (2009–2010), third (2011), and fourth grades (2012), using propensity score matching to generate 3 levels of eligibility. Although the immediate effect measured at mid-year of first grade on the Observation Survey was large (1.17), the effect by the end of first grade on the same measure was .51, and by third grade, the effect was .16 on the state reading test. The overall effect completely diminished by fourth grade, but it was significant (.35) for the most eligible students in reading, and for moderately eligible (.34) and most eligible students (.35) in writing. The sustained effect overall was present but diminished by third grade, and was sustained into fourth grade for those students at greater risk. The findings suggest that RR instruction should be better tailored to the initial literacy profiles of individual students to maximize the longevity of the effect for all participants.

One of the core factors leading to long-term risk for school failure is early literacy achievement. Without a targeted intervention, a student's relative ranking in reading proficiency changes little throughout elementary and middle school and low relative rankings are associated with not completing high school (Hernandez, 2011; Lesnick, Goerge, Smithgall, & Gwynne, 2010; Lloyd, 1978). These general patterns of reading achievement in American schooling underscore the need to intervene early for students who are having trouble reading in the early elementary grades.

Reading Recovery (RR), developed in the early 1970s by Marie Clay, is a short-term early literacy intervention designed to address the literacy needs of children who are struggling to read in the most critical period. To identify children for the intervention, first-grade students, excluding children who were retained in first grade, are rank ordered in terms of reading proficiency by the children's kindergarten teachers' (sometimes the first-grade teachers') assessment. The lowest 30% are tested with the Observation Survey of Early Literacy Achievement (OSELA; Clay, 2013) and the Slosson Oral Reading Test—R (Slosson & Nicholson, 2002) to identify the lowest achieving students in the cohort. The number of students selected depends on the number of available RR slots in the school, which typically is about 20% of the first-grade students at the school.

Although RR is one of the most researched programs in the world, the majority of evaluations of it have focused on the immediate effect of the intervention, rather than on its long-term impact, and most, if not all, of the studies that addressed the longer-term effects lacked methodological rigor. In this study, we examine the sustained effect of RR in Michigan by comparing the third- and fourth-grade state test scores of treatment and comparison students who represented three levels of need for the intervention.

RR is founded on Marie Clay's research on young children in the earliest phases of literacy acquisition while reading and writing meaningful connected text. First-grade children who are served by the intervention are offered 30-min daily lessons in a one-to-one instructional format by a teacher who has been highly trained in the program methods. Daily lessons consist of five components: rereading familiar books, taking a running record (without teacher support) on a book the student read the previous lesson, letter and word work in isolation, composing and constructing a written message, and introducing and supporting the student in reading a new book. The lessons address phonemic awareness, phonics, vocabulary, fluency, and comprehension within a system in which children learn to integrate meaning, structure, and letter-sound correspondences and to monitor, problem-solve, and self-correct as they read and write increasingly complex texts (Clay, 2005b).

The overall goals of the program are to (a) intervene early to accelerate the literacy achievement of the lowest performing learners in first grade so that they can continue to progress without further need of intensive support and to (b) identify the few children who, after having received a complete intervention, are referred for supplemental or longer-term support (Clay, 2001). Through the daily monitoring of a child's reading progress, the RR teacher gauges if the child has reached the average reading level of the school's first-grade class. Children can be discontinued from the intervention as early as 12 weeks if they reach the average level of their peers, but by 20 weeks, which is the maximum period of the intervention, children are recommended for supplemental or longer-term support if they do not reach such levels.

According to Clay (2005a), at the end of the intervention, children are expected to be on track to become effective silent readers who can continue to learn on their own, but who, like any student, require good classroom instruction and moderate motivational levels to sustain their growth. Clay maintained that students who received RR were not impervious to future reading struggles, and, indeed, she recommended that children be monitored closely for 3 years after treatment and be provided with refresher individualized instruction if their progress began to lag behind their peers.

One could argue that it is unnecessary to examine the impact of RR, or any other short-term intensive intervention, long after the treatment period ends, because a host of extraneous factors beyond the control of implementers may disrupt the later achievement trajectories of participants. Yet, a review of the espoused changes in students that are expected to result from RR make it clear that it is important to consider if the intentions of the program are fulfilled.

It is not clear to what extent Clay's posttreatment recommendations are followed, and it also is not clear if typical American classrooms offer the caliber of instruction that allow children the opportunity to stay on track with little supplemental help. For these reasons, it is vital to examine what happens to participants after the intervention in terms of their achievement in comparison to that of their peers.

Prior research on the sustained RR effect

Attempting to accurately estimate the longer-term effects of RR has proven to be a difficult task. Not only have most studies of RR's impact focused on the immediate effect, the quality of the research designs of studies that tracked children deteriorated from the immediate effect estimate to the follow-up time points. Many of the longer-term effect studies suffered from common methodological limitations, such as comparing treatment student outcomes to national norms rather than to similar needy students (e.g., Gapp, Zalud, & Pietrzak, 2009; Jesson & Limbrick, 2014), not ensuring fidelity of treatment implementation (e.g., Huggins, 1999; May, Sirinides, Gray, & Goldsworthy, 2016), and being hampered by severe attrition problems (e.g., May et al., 2016).

In their RR meta-analysis, D'Agostino and Harmey (2016) identified 16 immediate-impact studies that were deemed to be of sufficient methodological rigor. Five of the 16, or slightly over 30% of the studies, tracked children into second or third grade (or both). Overall, among the 16 studies, the average immediate effect was .59, but the second-grade effect was estimated to be 30 and the third-grade effect was −.01. In both cases, the 95% confidence intervals included zero, which resulted in the retention of the null hypothesis that there was no sustained effect even by second grade. Yet, both follow-up effects were based on four slightly different subsets of studies that yielded immediate effect estimates that were less than the point estimate derived from all 16 studies, which may have resulted in an underestimation of the true population longer-term effects.

Only one of the five studies (Pinnell, DeFord, & Lyons, 1988) was an experiment in which children were randomly assigned to treatment or control conditions, whereas two of the studies (Burroughs-Lange, 2008; Hurry & Sylvia, 2007) were quasi-experiments in which assignment was not random but statistical adjustments were performed to equate the groups. The other two studies (Clay, 2009; Huck & Pinnell, 1986) were not based on random assignment or statistical covariation, but pretest mean differences between treatment and control groups were within 5% of the pooled standard deviation.

A serious limitation of the studies, with the exception of Burroughs-Lange (2008) and Hurry and Sylvia (2007), is that follow-up effects were derived only from treatment children who successfully completed (e.g., discontinued) the intervention. Limiting the examination of the longer-term effects to those who reached sufficient achievement levels may be appropriate, in that it addresses the evaluation question: What is the prognosis for students who responded positively to the treatment? If the goal is to ascertain from an *intent to treat* perspective the long-term outcome for those who received a full treatment, however, excluding completers who did not successfully discontinue introduces a systematic bias in favor of the treatment group (in that there is no way to know which control students would have been successful had they had the treatment). The bias in favor of the treatment may have served as a counter effect to the underestimated immediate effect computed by D'Agostino and Harmey (2016).

Another methodological issue in studying the longer-term RR effects pertains to changes in instrumentation over time. Although Hiebert, Colt, Catto, and Gury (1992) and Slavin, Lake, Davis, and Madden (2011) expressed concern that effects based on the internal RR measure, the OSELA (Clay, 2013), likely lead to inflated impact estimates, almost half (45) of the 101 immediate effects from the 16 studies included in the D'Agostino and Harmey (2016) study were on OSELA measures, and half (eight) of the 16 effects from the five studies that provided follow-up effects were OSELA-driven.

The problem for examining the sustained effect is not whether the immediate or follow-up effects are based on internal or external measures, but rather the change in measures from the posttreatment to follow-up time points. D'Agostino and Harmey (2016) found that external measures yielded an immediate effect of .45, which is considerably less than the OSELA-based overall effect of .79. Indeed, the largest RR studies yielded an average immediate effect of .98 over four first-grade cohorts on the OSELA Total Score, whereas on an external measure (Iowa Test of Basic Skills Reading Total score) the immediate effect averaged .37 on the same four cohorts (May et al., 2016). Consequently, if the immediate effect is on OSELA measures, but the follow-up effects are externally based, an apparent diminished sustained effect may be at least partly due to instrumentation changes.

One experimental study not included in the D'Agostino and Harmey (2016) computation of longer-term effects (because students were followed only to the Fall of second grade) was by Pinnell, Lyons, DeFord, Bryk, and Seltzer (1994). In that study, the immediate effects on OSELA indicators were 1.50 for text reading and .65 on hearing and recording sounds in words. By the Fall of second grade follow-up, the effects on those measures had decayed to .75 and .35 respectively, revealing that instrumentation alone does not entirely explain diminished effects over time; even so, the sustained effects were much stronger than reported by D'Agostino and Harmey.

Yet another limitation with sustained-effect RR studies is that few have followed children for more than 2 years after treatment. A set of studies conducted in England, however, tracked the longer term effects 5 years past the treatment year. Taken together, the studies yielded mixed results regarding the longer-term impact of the intervention. Burroughs-Lange and Douëtil (2007) studied students who received RR and compared their progress with other first graders in the same schools and first graders in schools without RR. They found that RR students significantly outperformed students in both groups on the OSELA, British Ability Scales Word Reading Test II (BAS-II), and Word Reading and Phonics Skills (WRAPS). In fact, after controlling for beginning text level, all effect sizes on the OSELA and BAS-II for the RR students were greater than 0.70 with the largest effect size found for text reading level ($d = 2.10$). In a 1-year follow up, Burroughs-Lange (2008) administered the BAS-II and WRAPS to students who received RR the previous year and comparison students in schools without RR, and found that RR students performed significantly better than the comparison students on the BAS-II ($d = 0.74$) and WRAPS ($d = 0.79$).

Following students to the end of Year 4, Holliman and Hurry (2013; also see Hurry & Holliman, 2009) evaluated student progress on the UK National Curriculum (NC) assessment for RR students, students in similar schools, and comparison students in schools without RR. Multiple regression models indicated that RR student outperformed comparison students in non-RR schools, but performed similarly to students in RR schools. They argued that a contamination of RR in the RR schools accounted for the diminished effect. At the end of Year 6, Hurry (2012) reported a change in the outcomes on the NC assessment, with RR students and students in RR schools performing significantly better than the comparison group in non-RR schools. Yet, similar to previous findings, the RR students and students attending RR schools were not significantly different.

In terms of addressing the overarching question of the sustained effects of RR, the body of evidence overall, though derived from studies with a variety of methodological problems, suggests that effects diminish considerably by second grade and may disappear completely as soon as 2 years after the intervention year. The degree to which research design issues hinder a more accurate estimate of the effects remains unknown.

Purpose and goals of this study

Regardless of research quality and other differing features of past studies, all provided an estimate of sustained effects without consideration of initial student need for the intervention. Even studies that excluded nonsuccessful children did so in an ex post facto manner, and thus did not consider the degree of eligibility for RR before the treatment. During the i3 evaluation, which was the largest and most expansive evaluation of RR to date, more needy schools (based on average pretest values) were found to produce larger treatment effects, which may indicate that RR is more effective, at least in the short term, for students who initially are at the lowest achievement levels (May et al., 2016).

The typical or average child who is selected for RR in the Fall of first grade performs at the 14th percentile on the OS Total Score, but the 95% confident interval range of children selected nationally is from the first percentile to the 58th percentile (D'Agostino & Brownfield, 2016). This vast range of initial achievement does not reveal that RR schools are not identifying the most needy children, but instead reflects the great range in average achievement across schools. The standard RR selection protocol is to accept students who are among the lowest 20% of the first cohort within a school. Consequently, in more advantaged and higher achieving schools, some children performing in the lowest 20% within the school are actually performing above the 50th percentile nationally.

It is reasonable to expect that children selected for RR in higher performing schools are less likely to face the sociodemographic risk factors of students in lower performing schools (see Snow, Burns, & Griffin, 1998), but nonetheless are likely still at risk. Even though the students are in higher performing schools, they are at risk for failure within their school system if performing behind 80% of their local peers, and because they have fallen behind in schools with greater resources, they commonly do not have garden-variety reading issues but, instead, possess more persistent learning difficulties (see Stanovich, 1991).

Another reason RR may have been more effective in schools with initially lower test scores pertains to the degree to which RR teachers customized instruction. A number of instructional procedures are designed for children who are just beginning to emerge into conventional literacy. For example, instructional procedures help children to develop the alphabetic principle, to develop phonological awareness at the syllable level, to learn to identify all the letters in the alphabet, and to develop basic concepts about word and directionality. Children who enter the intervention performing at higher levels likely will not need these procedures and will make less progress during the intervention if teachers spend time teaching the basic concepts. This can happen if a teacher creates a uniform scope and sequence of instruction and fails to customize the lessons based on individual student needs.

This study was designed to address if the level of initial need for RR moderated not only the immediate effect, but the sustained effects, as well. We collected the third- and fourth-grade reading and writing state test scores for a cohort of first-grade students who received RR in Michigan during the 2009–2010 school year. We also collected the same test scores for a group of students at the RR schools that represented the population of first-grade students in the state. Using propensity score matching, we generated three levels of eligibility for the intervention and examined the treatment effects immediately after the intervention (midyear first grade), at the end of first grade, and at the beginning of both third and fourth grades. We hypothesized that effects would diminish over time across all students regardless of risk level, but that eligibility would moderate the sustained effect, with larger follow-up effects occurring among students that were at greater literacy risk.

Method

Participants

During the 2009–2010 school year, each school in the United States that offered RR was asked to administer the OSELA to two children in the first grade selected at random in the fall, midyear, and spring. Those students collectively are referred to as the *random sample*, and they serve to provide general population normative information to evaluate RR. In Michigan during 2009–2010, 185 RR schools collected random sample data, and thus served as the initial sampling frame for this study. Thirty-one of those schools were located in districts that did not agree to participate in the study, and thus, did not provide their students' third- or fourth-grade scores.

We asked the remaining 154 schools to provide the third- and fourth-grade reading and writing state test scores for first-grade students who either received RR or were in the random sample during the 2009–2010 school year. From 21 of those schools, it was not possible to obtain the state test scores on both RR and random sample students, and thus, including them in the final analytic sample would have led to an imbalance in school representation across the treatment and control groups. Thus, our final sample included 133 Michigan schools from which we could obtain the relevant test-score data. There were 328 students who received RR (treatment group) and 264 students who did not receive RR (control group). Only students in round one of RR (selected first) were included in the treatment group. Among those in the treatment group, there were 79% White, 13% African American, 5% Hispanic/Latino, 2% Asian, and 2% American Indian. About 8% of students were English Language Learners (ELL) and 27% were of minority status. Of the students in the control group, there were 74% White, 17% African American, 7% Hispanic/Latino, 1% Asian, and 1% American Indian. About 4% were ELL and 29% were of minority status. The median age of control students at entry to first grade was 6 years, 6 months (range: 5 years, 10 months to 7 years, 6 months); the median age of treatment students at the beginning of the school year was 6 years, 4 months (range: 5 years, 10 months to 7 years, 7 months).

Though the degree of student attrition was negligible at the 133 sample schools, we assumed that schools were not missing at random from the overall sampling frame. Hence, it was possible that districts that did not grant permission to schools to participate, or schools with extensive missing data, differed in important ways from the final sample schools. Because we had rather complete first-grade fall, mid-year, and spring OSELA scores on all students in Michigan during the 2009–2010 school year, we conducted a MANOVA to compare the mean scores of treatment and control students by subsample group (final sample, from nonparticipating districts, or schools with incomplete data) to ascertain if sampling bias likely existed.

The key comparisons of interest were across subsample group and the treatment by subsample interaction (the treatment main effect was irrelevant in terms of examining bias). There was no subsample mean difference effect across the fall, mid-year, and spring OSELA scores, $F(6, 1, 646) = 0.35$, $p = 0.91$, nor was there a treatment by subsample interaction, $F(6, 1, 646) = 0.45$, $p = 0.85$. The final, total sample did not statistically differ on the pretest, posttest, or the first follow-up OSELA from the students in nonparticipating districts or students in schools with incomplete data, and there was no statistical difference between treatment and control students across the three subsample groups.

Measures

The OSELA is an early literacy assessment that consists of six general tasks, or subtests: Letter Identification, Hearing and Recording Sounds in Words, Text Reading Level, Writing Vocabulary, the Ohio Word Test, and Concepts About Print (Clay, 2013). Each task yields a separate raw score, which have been combined by D'Agostino (2012) to produce an overall total score. The 2009–2010 Fall first-grade pretest OSELA total scores were used along with other variables to classify students into eligibility groups and as a covariate. We computed an immediate RR effect using the first-grade, mid-year OSELA total scores from the 2009–2010 school year. The spring first-grade OSELA scores from the year served as the first follow-up measure. Analyses were not conducted separately for the six task scores, because as Denton, Ciancio, and Fletcher (2006) have pointed out, distributional property limitations of the separate raw scores, such as floor and ceiling effects, render them unsuitable for evaluation purposes. Furthermore, the primary focus of this study was to examine intervention effects beyond first grade, so it was more efficient to utilize one combined OSELA measure for the three first-grade time points.

Students' Fall 2011 Michigan Education Assessment Program (MEAP) third-grade reading scale scores, Fall 2012 MEAP fourth-grade reading scale scores, and Fall 2012 MEAP fourth-grade writing scale scores were used to evaluate longer-term treatment effects. MEAP served as the statewide Michigan assessment system until the Fall of 2013, and was replaced with the M-STEP in the spring of the following school year. MEAP reading tests were administered in Grades 3 through 8, and MEAP writing exams were given in Grades 4 and 7 (hence, there was no third-grade MEAP writing exam). Because MEAP tests were administered in the Fall of each year, the tests covered the content standards and expectations of the previous grade level. Thus, the third-grade reading test covered second-grade content, and the fourth-grade exams covered third-grade content.

The third- and fourth-grade MEAP reading tests each contained 30 multiple-choice questions and one constructed-response item (Michigan Department of Education, 2013) that were based on a series of reading passages. In some cases, a pair of related passages was assessed with independent and cross-text items; other passages were presented independently with items. Across the two grades, reliability estimates of internal consistency from the 2012 and 2013 data ranged from .84 to .86, and empirical IRT reliabilities ranged from .79 to .83 (Michigan Department of Education, 2012, 2013). The MEAP fourth-grade writing test included 16 multiple-choice items and three constructed-response items, which include a response to a sample student writing product, a narrative writing prompt, and an informational writing prompt. Reliability estimates of internal consistency from the 2012 and 2013 data ranged from .86 to .87, and empirical IRT reliabilities ranged from .89 to .91 (Michigan Department of Education, 2012, 2013).

An ELL indicator, minority status, and Fall first-grade pretest OSELA scores were used to conduct propensity score matching.

Classification and statistical analyses

We used subclassification propensity score matching (Rosenbaum & Rubin, 1983) to adjust for pretreatment differences between the RR and random sample students. The goal of subclassification is to create homogenous subsets of students based on the conditional probability of being assigned to the treatment group given a vector of covariates. To classify students, we used logistic regression with group membership (0 = control, 1 = treatment) as the outcome variable, and the Fall pretest OSELA total scores, minority status (either African American or Hispanic), and ELL status as covariates. Table 1 presents the logistic regression results. All three variables significantly predicted group membership.

The predicted scores for each student from the logistic regression model served as the propensity scores, or likelihood of being assigned to the treatment based on the covariates in the model. The propensity score distribution was split into three subgroups based on natural distribution breaks. Students with scores from .99 to .89 were considered the most eligible group, those with scores from .88 to .76

Table 1. Summary of logistic regression analysis for covariates predicting treatment membership for Reading Recovery (n = 328) and control (n = 264) students.

Predictor	B	SE B	e^B
Fall OS total score	−.008*	.002	.99
ELL status	.427*	.186	1.53
Minority status	.145*	.045	1.16
Constant	3.20		

Note. e^B = exponentiated B. *$p < .001$.

were considered the moderately eligible group, and students with scores below .76 represented the least eligible group.

Table 2 provides the subsample counts and average OSELA pretest total scores for the three eligibility groups by treatment and control. As can be seen, there was reasonably good overlap between the treatment and control groups on the propensity score, especially given that RR targets the lowest 20% of first-grade students in each participating school. As expected, a greater proportion of treatment students were in the most eligible group, but there was a sizable most-eligible control group, indicating that many sample schools were not able to serve all eligible children (i.e., reach full coverage).

The average pretest scores of the treatment and control students were rather comparable among the most eligible students (i.e., within .11 standard deviation difference) but less comparable for the other two eligibility groups, as would be anticipated. The average score for the most eligible students was at the fourth percentile nationally; the mean score for the moderately eligible students was at the 15th percentile among treatment students and 17th percentile among controls. Among least eligible students, the RR student average of 413 was at the 35th percentile nationally, whereas the 462 average for least eligible control students was at the 70th percentile (D'Agostino, 2012). Disregarding eligibility level, the Fall average score for control students was at the 40th percentile nationally, revealing that sampled Michigan schools were slightly less proficient at the beginning of the school year compared to the population of RR schools nationally. Sampled RR students also were marginally less proficient than RR students across the country (12th percentile vs. 14th percentile, respectively), further indicating that the sample of schools was slightly lower achieving initially relative to schools that offered RR in the nation.

We conducted a MANCOVA with treatment-control group and eligibility group as between-subjects factors, the propensity score (probability of being eligible for the treatment) as a covariate, and the five posttests as outcome measures. Single-factor ANCOVA and follow-up tests served to interpret identified treatment effects.

Results

Before conducting group comparison statistics, we examined the correlations among the outcomes and OSELA pretest scores for both the random sample and RR students. The correlations by group are presented in Table 3. As expected, the correlations are stronger for the random sample than for RR likely due to less range restriction in the former group. The Fall first-grade OSELA scores were well

Table 2. Subsample counts and average OSELA pretest scores for the three eligibility groups by treatment and control.

		Treatment		Control	
Group	Propensity Scores	N	Fall OSELA Pretest (SD)	N	Fall OSELA Pretest (SD)
Least eligible	Below .76	49	413.39 (13.84)	122	461.72 (4.90)
Moderately eligible	.76 to .88	125	377.26 (9.73)	81	391.62 (10.89)
Most eligible	Above .88	154	342.63 (13.37)	61	341.23 (12.88)

Note. OSELA = Observation Survey of Early Literacy Achievement (Clay, 2013).

Table 3. Zero-order correlations among variables for random sample (n = 264) and Reading Recovery students (n = 328).

	Fall OSELA	Mid-Year OSELA	Spring OSELA	3rd MEAP Reading	4th MEAP Reading	4th MEAP Writing
Fall OSELA		.70*	.65*	.46*	.50*	.62*
Mid-Year OSELA	.21*		.80*	.58*	.50*	.56*
Spring OSELA	.45*	.58*		.44*	.38*	.52*
3rd MEAP Reading	.24*	.21*	.36*		.70*	.48*
4th MEAP Reading	.17*	.17*	.32*	.58*		.57*
4th MEAP Writing	.21*	.26*	.43*	.41*	.53*	

Note. Correlations above the diagonal are for the random sample. Correlations below the diagonal are for Reading Recovery students. OSELA = Observation Survey of Early Literacy Achievement (Clay, 2013); MEAP = Michigan Education Assessment Program (Michigan Department of Education, 2012, 2013). *$p < .01$.

correlated with the MEAP scores given the time gap of over 2 years between test administrations, indicating the need to control for pretest status. Indeed, Fall OSELA was more highly correlated with fourth-grade MEAP reading and writing than Spring OSELA for the random sample. Note that the OSELA correlations for both groups were equally as strong or stronger for MEAP writing as they were for MEAP reading.

Table 4 presents the MANCOVA results. As can be expected, even after controlling for the propensity score, there were significant differences across the eligibility groups on all outcomes. The treatment and control groups significantly differed on the immediate and first follow-up OSELA tests, and the third-grade MEAP reading test. Figure 1 displays the effect sizes between treatment and control on the five outcome measures. The immediate effect on the OSELA was 1.17, but it was reduced to .51 by spring. On the MEAP measures, the effect dropped to .16, and the effects in fourth grade were virtually zero. Note that the immediate effect of 1.17 was quite large and outside the confidence interval of .67 to .91 for OSELA measures. More recent OSELA immediate effects from the i3 scale up study, however, were in the .91 to 1.04 range, and thus were more comparable to the effect detected in this study.

There were treatment-by-eligibility interactions on all of the outcomes except third-grade MEAP. The treatment effect sizes by eligibility level are presented in Figure 2. It can be seen that the immediate effect measured on the midyear OSELA was sizable for all three eligibility groups. Follow-up contrasts and simple effects of the interaction revealed that, although a significant treatment and control difference existed at each eligibility level, the effect for most eligible students was significantly larger than for moderately eligible, $F(1,585) = 13.09$, $p < .001$, and least-eligible students, $F(1,585) = 8.64$, $p < .01$. Further, the effect for least eligible students was not significantly different than the effect for the moderately eligible students. At the time of the first follow-up, Spring of Grade 1, the same interaction pattern was evident, with the most eligible effect significantly larger than the moderately eligible, $F(1,585) = 5.89$, $p < .01$, and least eligible effect, $F(1,585) = 5.89$, $p < .01$, but the effects for the latter two eligibility groups did not differ significantly.

For fourth-grade MEAP reading, treatment students did not outperform control students among either the least or moderately eligible groups, but there was a significant treatment effect for most eligible students, $F(1, 585) = 9.81$, $p < .01$. Treatment students performed significantly worse on the

Table 4. Overall MANCOVA and single-factor ANCOVA test results.

			Single-Factor Tests				
Variable	MANCOVA	df	Mid-Year OSELA	Spring OSELA	3rd Grade Reading	4th Grade Reading	4th Grade Writing
Treatment (T)	61.25***	(1,585)	238.59***	33.80***	4.12*	.05	.41
Eligibility group (E)	4.53***	(2,585)	10.48***	6.65***	5.63**	11.82***	5.30**
T × E	4.50***	(2,585)	3.95*	3.12*	.20	3.62*	8.15***

Note. The cell values represent obtained F-statistic values for the omnibus MANCOVA and ANCOVA follow-up tests. ANCOVA = analysis of covariance; MANCOVA = multivariate analysis of covariance; OSELA = Observation Survey of Early Literacy Achievement (Clay, 2013). *$p < .05$. **$p < .01$. ***$p < .001$.

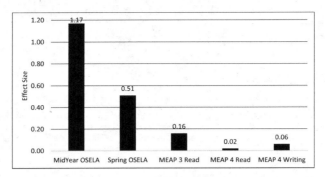

Figure 1. Treatment–control main effects. MEAP = Michigan Education Assessment Profile; OSELA = Observation Survey of Early Literacy Achievement (Clay, 2013).

fourth-grade MEAP writing test among least eligible students, $F(1,585) = 14.04$, $p < .001$, but there were positive treatment effects among moderately eligible, $F(1,585) = 17.55$, $p < .001$, and most eligible students, $F(1,585) = 9.30$, $p < .01$. The magnitude of the treatment effect did not differ significantly between moderately and most eligible students, but the treatment effect for least eligible students was significantly different compared to moderately eligible students, $F(1,585) = 10.14$, $p < .01$, and most-eligible students, $F(1,585) = 10.14$, $p < .01$.

Discussion

Most studies that have examined longer-term RR effects have not ascertained if the degree of eligibility moderates the RR immediate and sustained effect. After classifying each treatment and comparison student into one of three eligibility levels and using a propensity score as a covariate, we found a rather large immediate effect of 1.17 overall, which was larger than typically found in other RR studies. It stands to reason that the larger the immediate effect, the more likely a significant sustained effect would occur multiple years after the completion of the treatment, but, to our knowledge, no empirical work supports that assumption.

Our hypothesis, that the magnitude of the effect would diminish over time but that eligibility level would moderate the longer-term effect, mostly was supported by the findings, but the pattern of moderation was more convoluted than initially hypothesized. Eligibility level moderated the magnitude of the immediate effect, the first-grade Spring follow-up, and both fourth-grade MEAP measures, but not the third-grade MEAP. For the immediate and first follow-up effects, the treatment was significantly more effective for most eligible students compared to the other two eligibility groups, although

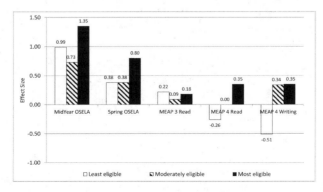

Figure 2. Treatment effects by three levels of eligibility. MEAP = Michigan Education Assessment Profile; OSELA = Observation Survey of Early Literacy Achievement (Clay, 2013).

the treatment effect decayed from mid-year to spring for the most eligible students. The treatment effect did not differ between the moderately and least eligible students at either time point.

In the Fall of third grade, the sustained effect remained significant but was reduced to .16 and eligibility level did not moderate the effect. By fourth grade, the sustained effect had diminished to a point of being statistically nonsignificant overall, but eligibility level again moderated the effect. The most eligible RR students significantly outperformed the most needy control students in both reading and writing, and indeed, the least eligible RR students were performing significantly worse than controls in writing. Among the most eligible students, the effects in both reading and writing MEAP were .35, which is not dramatically lower than the immediate RR effect for external measures (.45) found in the D'Agostino and Harmey (2016) meta-analysis, and which is greater than the most eligible third-grade MEAP reading effect (.18).

It is not entirely clear why the moderated effect apparently disappeared in third grade and reemerged in fourth. One obvious difference in MEAP testing was that the writing test was not administered in third grade, so it was possible that RR students had retained writing proficiency advantages from first to fourth grade. It also was possible that changes in the content domains between the third- and fourth-grade reading tests contributed to the apparent latent sustained effect for most eligible students. For example, the fourth-grade MEAP reading test may have emphasized more advanced comprehension in comparison to the third-grade MEAP reading test, and perhaps the most eligible RR students were better equipped to deal with the test content shift than their counterparts. It was not possible, however, to disaggregate the reading test by content strand or to locate detailed test specifications to test that hypothesis.

Some of the reduction in effects from first to third and fourth grade may have been due to an instrumentation effect. Yet, as D'Agostino and Harmey (2016) found, the typical immediate effect difference between the OSELA and external measures was on the magnitude of 1.75 (.79 compared to .45, respectively). The immediate effect in this study was over seven times the magnitude of the third-grade effect, so the difference cannot be completely attributed to changes in outcome measures. Administering the OSELA to children past second grade would not yield fruitful information regarding their literacy trajectories because the battery is designed to measure achievement during the emergent literacy window, so instrumentation change is unavoidable if the OSELA serves as the sole outcome to gauge immediate effects. Future research on the long-term effects of RR should entail the administration of external standardized measures that can suitably track growth from first to later grades.

The results, however, provided some evidence to support the interpretation that RR instruction is geared primarily toward the literacy needs of children who have the most pronounced struggles with basic literacy concepts. Those students, who mainly function in the first decile initially, gain the most from the intervention in the short term, which appears to pay dividends later on in relation to comparison students who also experience the greatest barriers to learning how to read. Results also support the assertion that the focus of the intervention is on cultivating a generative reading processing system that, over time, improves with practice and enables the reader to read increasingly more complex texts. It seems, then, that the most needy students, those with the most primitive literacy processing at the beginning of the intervention, may be more sensitive and responsive to intensive reading instruction.

RR does not have scripted or uniform instruction for all students; even though teachers follow the same lesson components, they decide which elements of the reading process to emphasize, what texts to read, and how much support to give students as they problem-solve. It is reasonable to expect variation in teacher expertise in terms of adapting the lesson framework to fit the needs of individual students. The findings of this study point to the need to increase the overall expertise of RR teachers in the complex decision-making that characterizes RR instruction, particularly for students who enter the intervention, not performing at the lowest levels, but who have some print awareness and may have developed idiosyncratic ways of approaching print.

Besides focusing on initial achievement levels and instructional needs upon intake and during the RR intervention, future research is needed to better discern the literacy achievement profiles upon exit from RR that provide students the greatest chance to maintain their growth trajectories as they matriculate through the grades. As Holliman, Hurry, and Bodman (2014) found, certain attributes that were measured at exit from RR, such as proficiency in reading connected text (as measured by text reading level) and reading comprehension, better predicted later reading and writing achievement long-term compared to other OSELA tasks and phonological processing. Not all children leave the intervention with the same profile of achievement, and we need to better understand what students need to be able to do to maintain their literacy progress in future years and to be no more vulnerable to risk factors than the average student.

Yet even for the most at-risk children, the longer-term effect of RR is less than that of the intervention's immediate impact, which suggests that RR is not an inoculation against social and educational factors that may impinge on students' literacy development. Schools cannot expect to provide RR in first grade and not concern themselves about the future learning trajectories of participating students. The results of this study support Clay's (2005a) advice to educators that after the treatment, children should be monitored for multiple years, be provided with high-quality classroom instruction, and be provided supplemental support if their achievement rates start to decline. RR probably is best offered within a more comprehensive school model in which instruction is better aligned between intensive and classroom practices, and where students are tracked continuously to best meet their needs.

Perhaps the most demanding challenge of conducting research on the longer-term effects of a program is the difficulty of retaining participants over time. We could not locate the state test scores for a number of students, most likely due to student mobility. Although we found that attrition did not lead to a final sample that differed from dropped students in terms of first-grade OSELA scores, and that we were able to retain about 72% of the initial sampling frame, it was possible that students and schools in this study differed in other ways from the population of RR Michigan schools and students in 2009–2010. Furthermore, it would have been more methodologically sound to conduct multilevel analysis at the school level to consider clustering effects, but because there were only two random sample students and about three RR students per school, it was not possible to conduct propensity matching within the schools. We also were not able to obtain other information about the students, such as whether any control students received supplemental interventions, or whether RR was the only intervention provided to treatment students from first to fourth grade.

To more accurately study the longer-term effects of the intervention, more rigorous studies should be designed and implemented that would entail randomly assigning children from various strata of initial achievement to either receive RR or not, and to properly track the children over multiple years with a measure designed to capture literacy growth. There is an ethical concern when a treatment known to be effective is purposively withheld from individuals who would benefit greatly from the intervention, but many schools do not have enough teachers to properly serve all eligible children, and at these partial coverage schools, assigning children at random to the treatment or control conditions may represent a fair system of allocating resources. Until such studies are conducted, the inferences drawn from the extant literature will be too tenuous to conclude with an adequate degree of certainty that RR has a lasting effect.

References

Burroughs-Lange, S. (2008). *Comparison of literacy progress of young children in London Schools: A RR Follow-Up Study*. London, UK: Institute of Education. Retrieved from https://www.ioe.ac.uk/Comparison_of_Literacy_Progress_of_Young_Children_in_London_Schools_-_A_Reading_Recovery_Follow_up_Study_.pdf

Burroughs-Lange, S., & Doüetil, J. (2007). Literacy progress of young children from poor urban settings: A Reading Recovery comparison study. *Literacy Teaching and Learning, 12*(1), 19–46.

Clay, M. M. (2001). *Change over time in children's literacy development*. Portsmouth, NH: Heinemann.

Clay, M. M. (2005a). *Literacy lessons designed for individuals, Part one: Why, when, and how?* Portsmouth, NH: Heinemann.

Clay, M. M. (2005b). *Literacy lessons designed for individuals, Part two: Teaching procedures*. Portsmouth, NH: Heinemann.

Clay, M. M. (2009). The Reading Recovery research reports. In B. Watson & B. Askew (Eds.), *Boundless horizons: Marie Clay's search for the possible in children's literacy* (pp. 37–100). Rosedale, NZ: Pearson Education.

Clay, M. M. (2013). *An observation survey of early literacy achievement* (3rd ed.). Portsmouth, NH: Heinemann.

D'Agostino, J. V. (2012). *U.S. norms and correlations for An Observation Survey of Early Literacy Achievement* (Report No. 2012–04). Columbus, OH: International Data Evaluation Center.

D'Agostino, J. V., & Brownfield, K. (2016). *Reading Recovery and Descubriendo la Lectura national report 2014–2015* (Report No. 2016-01). Columbus, OH: International Data Evaluation Center.

D'Agostino, J. V., & Harmey, S. (2016). An international meta-analysis of Reading Recovery. *Journal of Education for Students Placed At Risk, 21,* 29–46.

Denton, C. A., Ciancio, D., & Fletcher, J. (2006). Validity, reliability, and utility of the Observation Survey of Early Literacy Achievement. *Reading Research Quarterly, 41,* 8–34. doi:10.1598/RRQ.41.1.1

Gapp, S. G., Zalud, G., & Pietrsak, D. (2009). End of intervention Reading Recovery decisions and subsequent achievement. *Reading Improvement, 46,* 9–18.

Hernandez, D. J. (2011). *Double jeopardy: How third-grade reading skills and poverty influence high school graduation.* Baltimore, MD: Annie E. Casey Foundation.

Hiebert, E. H., Colt, J. M., Catto, S. L., & Gury, E. C. (1992). Reading and writing of first-grade students in a restructured Chapter 1 program. *American Educational Research Journal, 29,* 545–572. doi: 10.3102/0002831202900354

Holliman, A. J., & Hurry, J. (2013). The effects of Reading Recovery on children's literacy progress and special educational needs status: A three-year follow-up study. *Educational Psychology, 33,* 719–733. doi:10.1080/01443410.2013.785048

Holliman, A. J., Hurry, J., & Bodman, S. (2016). Children's reading profiles on exiting the Reading Recovery programme: Do they predict sustained progress? *Journal of Research in Reading, 39,* 1–18. doi:10.1111/1467-9817.12041

Huck, C. S., & Pinnell, G. S. (1986). *The Reading Recovery project in Columbus, Ohio, Vol. 1 Pilot year 1984–1985.* Columbus, OH: Ohio State University.

Huggins, R. (1999). *Longitudinal study of the Reading Recovery program: 1994–1998.* Detroit, MI: Detroit Public Schools, Office of Research, Evaluation, and Assessment. (ERIC Document Reproduction Service No. ED 430067).

Hurry, J. (2012). *The impact of Reading Recovery five years after intervention.* London, UK: University of London, Institute of Education. Retrieved from http://www.ioe.ac.uk/Research_Home/Hurry-London-Follow-Up-2012-Report-December.pdf

Hurry, J., & Holliman, A. (2009). *The impact of Reading Recovery three years after intervention.* London, UK: University of London, Institute of Education. Retrieved from https://www.ioe.ac.uk/PHD_JH_Reading_Recovery_report_2009.pdf

Hurry, J., & Sylva, K. (2007). Long-term outcomes of early reading intervention. *Journal of Reading Research, 30,* 227–248. doi: 10.1111/j.1467-9817.2007.00338.x

Jesson, R., & Limbrick, L. (2014). Can gains from early literacy interventions be sustained? The case of Reading Recovery. *Journal of Research in Reading, 37,* 102–117. doi:10.1111/1467-9817.12017

Lesnick, J., Goerge, R., Smithgall, C., & Gwynne, J. (2010). *Reading on grade level in third grade: How is it related to high school performance and college enrollment?* Chicago, IL: Chapin Hall at the University of Chicago.

Lloyd, D. N. (1978). Prediction of school failure from third-grade data. *Educational and Psychological Measurement, 38,* 1193–1200. doi:10.1177/001316447803800442

May, H., Sirinides, P., Gray, A., & Goldsworthy, H. (2016). *Reading Recovery: An evaluation of the four-year i3 scale-up.* Philadelphia, PA: Consortium for Policy Research in Education. doi:10.12698/cpre.2014.rr79

Michigan Department of Education. (2012). *Michigan educational assessment program: Technical report 2011–2012.* Lansing, MI: Bureau of Assessment and Accountability, Michigan Department of Education.

Michigan Department of Education. (2013). *Michigan educational assessment program: Technical Report 2012–2013.* Lansing, MI: Bureau of Assessment and Accountability, Michigan Department of Education.

Pinnell, G. S., DeFord, D. E., & Lyons, C. A. (1988). *Reading Recovery: Early intervention for at-risk first graders (Educational Research Service Monograph).* Arlington, VA: Educational Research Service. (ERIC Document Reproduction Service No. ED303790).

Pinnell, G. S., Lyons, C. A., DeFord, D. E., Bryk, A., & Seltzer, N. (1994). Comparing instructional models for the literacy education of high risk first graders. *Reading Research Quarterly, 29,* 8–39. doi:10.2307/747736

Rosenbaum, P. R., & Rubin, D. B. (1983). The central role of the propensity score in observational studies for causal effects. *Biometrika, 70,* 41–55. doi:10.1017/cbo9780511810725.016

Slavin, R., Lake, C., Davis, S., & Madden, N. (2011). Effective programs for struggling readers: A best-evidence synthesis. *Educational Research Review, 6,* 1–26. doi:10.1016/j.edurev.2010.07.002

Slosson, R. L., & Nicholson, C. L. (2002). *Slosson Oral Reading Test–revised 3.* East Aurora, NY: Slosson Educational.

Snow, C. E., Burns, M. S., & Griffin, P. (Eds.). (1998). *Preventing reading difficulties in young children.* Washington, DC: National Academies Press. doi:10.17226/6023

Stanovich, K. E. (1991). Discrepancy definitions of reading disability: Has intelligence led us astray? *Reading Research Quarterly, 26,* 7–29. doi:10.2307/747729

Differences in the Early Writing Development of Struggling Children Who Beat the Odds and Those Who Did Not

Sinéad J. Harmey and Emily M. Rodgers

ABSTRACT
We used mixed methods to examine differences in the early writing development of children, identified as at risk of literacy difficulties, in the context of Reading Recovery (RR). From an extant dataset of 24 children, we identified those who made fast progress ($n = 6$) and those who did not ($n = 8$). We studied change over time in the sources of information they used and problem-solving actions they took over the course of the intervention. We developed a writing rubric to analyze videos of writing interactions (280 min) and written messages ($N = 674$). Results demonstrated that the fast-progress group had higher end of intervention ratings for multiple dimensions of writing. HLM analysis showed that the fast-progress group had higher rates of growth in their use of sources of information (spelling and letter-sound relationships) and observable problem-solving behaviors. Fast- and slow-progress groups did not differ in what they wrote but, for both groups, dips in legibility coincided with increased linguistic complexity. By juxtaposing descriptions of writing development for both groups, results provide useful information for instruction and intervention.

Learning to write is a critical component of becoming literate (cf. Clay, 2001; Fitzgerald & Shanahan, 2000), and the development of strong writing skills plays an important role in enhancing later reading development (Graham & Hebert, 2012; Graham et al., 2012). Given its importance, it is somewhat surprising that we know so little, comparatively speaking, about how early writing development proceeds. Indeed, descriptions of literacy development are much more coherent and diverse in terms of early and skilled reading development than early and skilled writing development (Beard, Myhill, Riley, & Nystrand, 2009).

There is, according to Tolchinsky (2016), a critical gap in extant research about early writing development that occurs during the period when children learn to put words into sentences and when they produce cohesive texts, or move into conventional literacy (typically the first two years of formal schooling). In terms of schooling, McNaughton (2011a) described this period as critical because children, who are working hard to learn how to read and write, are at risk of experiencing difficulties that can affect progress in the long term (p. 3).

It is reasonable to expect, therefore, that if we could better describe the writing development of young children identified as at risk of later literacy difficulties during the first years of formal schooling, and the differences between those who beat the odds by catching up with their peers and those who do not, that we could use that awareness to optimize learning and instruction for writing (Beard et al.,

Color versions of one or more of the figures in the article can be found online at www.tandfonline.com/hjsp.

2009). It also seems reasonable to expect, because of the reciprocal nature that appears to exist between early writing and reading development that improving writing instruction will also have a positive impact on reading development.

The purpose of this study, therefore, is to describe the differences in the early writing development of children, identified as at risk of later literacy difficulties. Specifically, we analyze differences between two groups of children, both of whom started first grade at very low levels of literacy achievement and were selected for Reading Recovery (RR) (Clay, 2005), but who either (a) beat the odds by making fast progress and catching up with their peers by the end of the 20-week intervention, or (b) made slow progress, did not respond well to the intervention and remained far behind their peers in terms of literacy learning. Like McGee, Kim, Nelson, and Fried (2015) who studied change in reading, we describe observed changes in what young writers learn to do and the sources of information that they learn to use while writing a short message with a teacher's help. Findings about the quantitative and qualitative differences between the two groups of children, both identified as at risk of later literacy difficulties, in the context of an early literacy intervention, will lend to our understanding about writing development at a critical period.

Promoting early writing development to beat the odds of literacy failure

Once children fall behind in literacy, they are unlikely to catch up; early failure means continued failure for most young children (Juel, 1988). The critical need to intervene early has been well established to change predictions of failure that come with early literacy difficulties (Vellutino et al., 1996).

Knowing more about how writing proceeds and how change differs for children identified as at risk of later literacy difficulties is important because the writing process, and the component skills involved in writing, appear to play a central role in the prevention of later literacy difficulties. Teaching the writing process and increasing the amount of writing that children do can improve children's reading comprehension (Graham & Hebert, 2012). Indeed, Graham and Hebert found that spelling instruction can improve both word reading and reading fluency, and teaching sentence construction can improve oral reading fluency. Moreover, invented spelling has been shown to promote phonological and orthographic knowledge and facilitate later reading development (Ouellette & Sénéchal, 2008, p. 899; 2017). It has even been documented that the development of fine motor skills involved in writing is causally linked to decoding skills development (Suggate, Pufke, & Stoeger, 2016).

Characterizing early writing development

Models of early writing development that provide metaphors about how writing develops are scant and certainly less well developed than those about reading (Puranik & Lonigan, 2014); nevertheless, existing models are useful in that they identify predictors of later literacy achievement. Wagner et al.'s (2011) model of early writing development identified five factors that explained differences in student growth, including handwriting fluency, message complexity (t-units and syntactic density), and macro-organization variables, as well as (but to a lesser extent) spelling and punctuation. Other models (cf. Hayes & Berninger, 2009; Juel, Griffith, & Gough, 1985) focus on identifying the component skills of writing and empirical studies framed by these models tend to use cross-sectional designs to explicate the relationship between factors like name writing (Bloodgood, 1999; Both-de Vries & Bus, 2008; Cabell, Justice, Zucker, & McGinty, 2009; Haney, 2002) or letter writing (Puranik, Lonigan, & Kim, 2011) involved in early writing development. Studies such as these are important in that they help to identify the factors that are related to literacy success but they do not tell us what develops nor how these factors change over the course of development, information useful to inform instruction.

Learning to write involves the orchestration of knowledge about letters, letter-sound associations, orthography, words, concepts about print, sentence, and text structure while simultaneously demanding control of working memory, self-regulation, monitoring of the accuracy of the written message (MacArthur & Graham, 2016). It is dependent on fine motor skills and transcription fluency (McCutchen, 1996). Similarly, Clay (2001) suggested that "within the directional constraints of print"

(p. 1) young readers and writers learn to draw on multiple sources of information as they problem-solve the task of reading or composing text. These sources of information could include oral language, letter-sound associations, letter shapes, orthography, grammatical knowledge, and semantics.

Moreover, it has been posited that children must learn to take problem-solving actions when they encounter difficulty while writing (Clay, 2001). These problem-solving actions include searching for more information, monitoring, and cross-checking sources of information, and can be inferred by observable behaviors like rereading, pausing, and self-correction (Boocock, McNaughton, & Parr, 1998). The development of these problem-solving actions has been characterized as change from simple to complex over time, but proceeding along different paths of development for each child (Clay, 2001). As such, an examination of writing development requires attention both to what children write and how they write it.

Measuring early writing development

Several researchers have used Siegler's (1996) overlapping wave perspective to describe how changes occur in components of the writing process (Jones, 1998; Rittle-Johnson & Siegler, 1999; Sharp, Sinatra, & Reynolds, 2008; Yaden & Tardibueno, 2004). Taken together, the findings from these studies demonstrate that writing development can be described as proceeding in overlapping waves and not in a uniform manner across subjects. There are three assumptions about development from an overlapping waves perspective: (1) Children approach tasks in a variety of ways, (2) these ways of thinking or approaches compete with one another until they reach a point of stability, and (3) development involves gradual change over time (Chen & Siegler, 2000). Thus, from this viewpoint, knowing more about the path, rate, and variability of change is important.

The present study

A gap in the research, and one that we intend to address in this paper, is that researchers have tended to focus on identifying specific factors regarding early written products (such as spelling or concept of word) that predict later literacy success rather than attending to a broad spectrum of early writing behaviors in addition to children's written messages. In addition, few researchers have tried to explicate the differences in changes in writing behaviors when development accelerates or goes awry during the critical period when children emerge into conventional literacy. Our paper attempts to address these gaps in that we study change over time in what children write and how they wrote it, for children making fast progress and for those whose progress appears to have gone awry in the context of a writing intervention. The results hold the potential to provide valuable information for those who work with children at risk of later literacy difficulties.

Study purpose and research questions

The purpose of this study was to describe differences in the writing development of children's (1) use of sources of information (oral language, letter/sound relationships, spelling, and use of directional rules) (2) strategic activities inferred by observable writing behaviors (monitoring, searching, self-correction, and fluency) and (3) written messages (linguistic complexity and legibility). In particular, we sought to describe how change differed for children classified as making fast or slow progress in written production in the context of an early literacy intervention. The questions that guided our inquiry were:

1. How do the sources of information that children use as they write with a teacher change over time and how does this change differ for children who made fast or slow progress in the context of an early literacy intervention?
2. How do the strategic activities, inferred from children's observable revision behaviors as they write with a teacher, change over time and how does this change differ for children who make fast or slow progress in the context of an early literacy intervention?

3. How does the linguistic complexity and legibility of children's written messages change over time and how does this change differ for children who made fast or slow progress in the context of an early literacy intervention?

Context for the study: Reading Recovery lessons

At the beginning of first grade, the children in this study were identified as the lowest achieving by their schools in terms of their literacy achievement on the Observation Survey of Early Literacy Achievement (OSELA) (Clay, 2013) and thus, as at risk of later literacy difficulties. They were subsequently provided with a short-term early literacy intervention, RR (Clay, 2005). RR is a one-to-one daily intervention that occurs over a period of no more than 20 weeks. The efficacy of RR has been demonstrated in a multi-site randomized controlled study by May et al. (2015) who determined that effect of RR on treatment students was .47 relative to a national sample of their first-grade peers on a standard measure of reading ability. For this reason, we thought the context appropriate, as we could reasonably expect to see accelerated changes for some students and little change for others over a short period.

The daily lesson involves reading, letter and word work, and a writing component. We focused solely on the writing component, typically lasting about 10 min each lesson. While Clay (2001) described writing as important in terms of its contribution to learning to read, she also stated it was important in its own right (p. 18) and is, thus, an essential component in the RR lesson, conducted not just to serve reading. During this part of the lesson, the student composes and writes a short message of about one to two sentences with teacher support (Clay, 2005). The message may be about any topic: the book that was just read in the lesson, something exciting that happened to the student, or a topic that interests the child (cf. DeFord, 1994). It is expected that children will learn how to compose and construct messages, form letters, learn to attend to directionality of print, and develop phonemic and orthographic awareness.

Clay and Cazden (1990) described the teacher's role in this part of the lesson as making deliberate teaching decisions to increase the child's accessibility to the task of writing a simple message, offering more or less help as needed to compose and record the message. Clay (2005) noted that, in RR lessons, the "child learns to bring together …the ideas, the message (which must be his own), the search for ways to record it, the monitoring of the message production, and the reading of what he has recorded" (p. 52).

The setting therefore was suitable for our study as all the teachers used similar instructional techniques to support writing and message intent was free to vary and not controlled by the teacher. Such a setting is more likely to reflect actual writing development than when children are writing controlled tasks (Dyson, 1983). Finally, given the documented evidence of student responsiveness to the intervention, it was reasonable to expect that some children would make accelerated progress from low levels of achievement while others would not, thereby providing us with a useful context to study variability in the early writing development of children identified as at risk of later literacy difficulties.

Method

We used mixed methods to address questions about how learning changes over time. For Research Question 3 we used a microgenetic design. This design is used to understand the mechanisms of change (Flynn, Pine, & Lewis, 2006) and to reveal how children come to know rather than "what they know" (Granott & Parziale, 2002, p. 12). Consequently, the method requires a high density of observations, repeated frequently over a period of rapid change, that are analyzed intensely (Siegler, 2006). The method is resource intensive which results in lower numbers of participants. An affordance of the method, however, is a picture of development at individual level that is detailed as opposed to just snapshots of development.

We used an extant dataset that contained records for 24 students. This dataset contained 1,050 written messages and 48 videos (totaling 450 min of instruction) taken at several points during the intervention. The dataset comprised data for 24 students who attended 22 schools in a large urban city in a midwestern state of the United States. In 23 of the 24 schools over 80% of the school population were considered economically disadvantaged. Seventeen of the schools did not meet the state's quality indicator of having 80% of children scoring proficient or above in reading and math (Harmey, 2015). The schools were ethnically diverse.

Participants

Students

We used Writing Vocabulary (WV), a task of the OSELA (Clay, 2013) to identify students in the two groups. First, we selected all children whose Fall WV score would put them at or below the 20th percentile compared to a random sample of their peers at the beginning of first grade ($n = 14$). The remaining 10 students started the program above the 20th percentile and, thus, were not considered for inclusion in the study.

To form the groups, we selected children whose WV score at the end of first grade on the OSELA was at or above the 30th percentile ($n = 6$) as those who made fast progress and those whose exit WV remained below the 20th percentile ($n = 8$) as slow-progress students (see Table 1). There were three boys and three girls in the high-progress group, only one of whom spoke English as an additional language. There were five boys and three girls in the low-progress group, only one of whom spoke English as an additional language.

The fast-progress group's mean pre-intervention WV score was 3.5 ($SD = 1.97$), placing them, on average, at the 5th percentile. Their post-intervention mean WV score was 39.83 ($SD = 6.05$), placing them, on average, at the 45th percentile. The slow-progress group's mean pre-intervention WV score was 6.38 ($SD = 2.13$), placing them, on average at or below the 11th percentile. Their post-intervention mean WV score was 24.63 ($SD = 3.16$), placing them, on average, at the 12th percentile at the end of the intervention. It could be suggested that this low-progress group made typical progress, as their percentile rank remained relatively the same. We argue that, given that the children were receiving daily, intensive instruction, this progress is slow as one should expect the children to make fast progress and to catch up with their peers.

An independent t-test demonstrated a significant difference between the fast ($M = 3.5$, $SD = 1.97$) and slow progress groups' ($M = 6.38$, $SD = 2.13$) means at the beginning of the intervention, $t_{(12)} = 2.57$, $p < .05$. It is worth noting, however, that it was the group that made fast progress whose means scores were initially lower than the group that made slow progress. By the end of the intervention, there was a statistically significant difference between the fast ($M = 39.83$, $SD = 6.05$) and slow progress groups' ($M = 24.63$, $SD = 3.16$) mean WV scores, $t_{(12)} = 6.14$, $p < .0001$, $d = 3.15$. The difference in means, on this occasion, was in favor of the fast-progress group.

Table 1. Slow- (n = 8) and fast- (n = 6) progress groups' demographics, pre-/post-intervention and difference between writing vocabulary* scores.

	Race/Ethnicity	Language Spoken at Home	Pre-intervention		Post-intervention		Difference	
			Raw Score	Percentile	Raw Score	Percentile	Raw Score	Percentile
			Slow Progress					
Josh	Black	English	4	5	29	18	+25	+13
Katie	Black	English	8	16	29	18	+21	+2
Hailey	Black	English	7	13	25	12	+18	−1
Ethan	Black	English	4	5	26	13	+22	+8
Tyler	Black	English	5	8	23	9	+18	+1
Gabriel	White	English	5	8	22	8	+17	0
Maria	Hispanic	Spanish	9	20	22	8	+13	−12
Robert	Black	English	9	20	21	7	+12	−13
Group Average			6.38	11.88	24.63	11.63	18.25	−.25
			Fast Progress					
Paul	Hispanic	Spanish	4	5	49	69	+45	+64
Courtney	White	English	2	2	46	65	+44	+63
Jake	Black	English	2	2	37	38	+35	+36
Daniel	White	English	2	2	36	35	+34	+33
Emma	Black	English	4	5	35	33	+31	+28
Courtney	White	English	7	13	36	35	+29	+22
Group Average			3.5	4.83	39.83	45.83	36.33	41.17

*Raw score is the number of words written in 10 min.

Teachers

The 14 students were taught by 12 teachers who were in the initial professional-development year to become RR teachers. Two children in the slow-progress group (Josh and Robert) were taught by the same teacher. Although the teachers were new to the RR intervention, all were at least mid-career elementary school teachers with an average of 15 years' teaching experience between them. They were all female; three were Black and nine were White.

Sources of data

Sources of data included videos and writing samples of the writing component of the RR lesson for the children in our study. The videos were taken at Week 5 (first observation) and the last week (final observation) of the intervention, and totaled 28 videos, or approximately 280 min of writing instruction. All videos were checked for fidelity to the RR framework by the first author, who had expertise in RR. Each written message for the 14 students was analyzed for this study ($N = 674$ messages). As described earlier, teachers are expected to include a writing component in each student's daily lesson. The teacher helps the student compose a short message of 1–2 sentences on one sheet of paper, while another sheet serves as a practice page where the teacher can teach the student strategies for spelling unfamiliar words (using phonemic awareness, orthographic awareness, rimes, morphemes, or sight words).

Measures

In order to address our research questions, we used Clay's (2013) OSELA to select students and a researcher-designed rubric to analyze the videos and writing documents.

An Observation Survey of Early Literacy Achievement

The OSELA (Clay, 2013) has six tasks that include word reading, text reading, word writing, phonological encoding, and conceptual awareness about print. In the United States, a total score is available which has been found to provide an effective means of screening for later literacy difficulties (D'Agostino, Rodgers, & Mauck, 2017). The National Center for Response to Intervention [NCRTI] (2010) reviewed the OSELA and stated that there was convincing evidence in terms of the reliability, validity, and classification accuracy of the assessment. The NCRTI also stated that the assessment had broad generalizability. In fact, of all the screening assessments reviewed by the NCRTI, the OSELA was rated highly across five categories, namely classification accuracy, generalizability, reliability, validity and disaggregated reliability, validity, and classification for diverse populations.

In our study, we used two of the writing tasks from the OSELA. We used Hearing and Recording Sounds in Words (HRSW) and WV to establish the validity of our rubric. We used the WV task to identify our groups. For the WV task the child is provided with a blank page and asked to write as many words as possible in 10 min. Each correctly spelled word receives one point. In the HRSW task, one of five alternate forms of a sentence is read aloud and the child is asked to write the sentence. Each phoneme correctly recorded accurately receives a score with a maximum score of 37. The OSELA (Clay, 2013) is used in many countries and estimates of reliability and validity from various studies have been provided. The test-retest reliability estimates for WV range between .62 and .97. The inter-rater reliability estimate for WV is .93 (p. 168). The test-retest reliability of HRSW ranges between .64 - .94 with alpha coefficients ranging between .92 and .96.

The Early Writing Observational Rubric

The Early Writing Observational Rubric (EWOR) comprised two parts: (a) ratings to judge the student's writing behaviors during the composition and writing of the message and (b) written message ratings to judge the legibility and complexity of the finished message.

Writing behaviors

In line with Clay's (2001) literacy processing theory, the observational element of the EWOR is divided into two subsections; (i) Using and (ii) Doing. *Using* refers to the sources of information or knowledge used to write continuous text. *Doing* refers to the child's observed behaviors that implied strategic processing or problem-solving actions. Using the rubric, the rater is asked to observe the child's actions as they are observed to write and to consider how the child moves from not initiating a particular behavior to self-initiating use of sources of knowledge or a problem-solving action in a fast and efficient manner. Items are rated on a scale of 0 (no observation of writing behavior) to 3 (observed independence in writing behavior) with a maximum possible score of 30 (see Figure 1). Essentially, along all items the rater considers if: (0) The teacher was observed to contribute all the information or assume responsibility for the action; (1) The child was observed to contribute this information with high support or demonstrated the behavior on at least one occasion; (2) The child mostly contributed this information with minimal help; or (3) The child consistently contributed the information or demonstrated the behavior with efficiency.

The items in the Using section of the EWOR include children's use of language to communicate a meaningful message (Harris, Fitzsimons, & McKenzie, 2004), use of letter-sound knowledge, use of orthographic information, concept of word, directionality, and number of words written independently. The Doing section has four items. The first item, "rereading as if to search for more information," refers to whether the child relied on the teacher to tell the next word, used a word already written or read, or reread the sentence up to the point of the last written word or letter. Taken together, these observable behaviors could infer that the child was searching for more information (meaning, structure, or orthographic information) (Boocock et al., 1998) to write the message. The second item, "rereading as if to monitor for accuracy," refers to whether children reread the accuracy of what was already written. This observable behavior might suggest that the child was actively monitoring what he wrote, and cross-checking what was written down with what was intended (Chanquoy, 2009). The third item in this section is self-correction. For this item, the rater must consider whether the writer examines the text produced and corrects, or revises, the text written (Chanquoy, 2009, p. 80). The fourth and final item asks the rater to consider the fluency or speed at which the child wrote letters, words, and text.

	Item	Score of 0	Score of 1	Score of 2	Score of 3	Total
U S I N G	Use of Language to Compose	Did not initiate/struggled to compose message without high support or was told what to write.	Slow to initiate composition of a simple message. Needed high support to construct message.	Exhibited control of parts of the conversation and composition. With support expanded message.	In control of the conversation/had a message ready to write. Composing was fluent and was flexible to make changes on the run.	
	Use of Orthographic Information	Did not demonstrate any awareness of orthographic features of words. Teacher contributed information.	Demonstrated some awareness of the orthographic features of words with prompting.	For many words, demonstrated some awareness of the orthographic features of words with minimal help.	Demonstrated awareness of the orthographic features of words and words were mostly spelled accurately and with efficiency	
	Use of Letter-sound Knowledge	Did not initiate slow articulation of words. Needed support to say word slowly, hear, and record sounds.	With prompting, could say word slowly and hear and record some initial sounds and dominant consonants with support.	Initiated slow articulation and heard and recorded phonemes in words from beginning to end with minimal support.	Initiated slow analysis of words independently and accurately (sometimes using vocalization to break a word apart or silently).	
	Use of Writing Vocabulary	Did not write any words independently.	Wrote one word independently. Process was slow. On all other occasions required support.	Wrote some words independently and with some speed with minimal support.	Wrote all words quickly, efficiently, and independently without support.	
	Use of Print Knowledge	Did not initiate placing spaces between words and needed constant direction.	Sometimes initiated making spaces between words but still needed support.	Spaced words correctly with minimal intervention.	Put spaces between words efficiently and needed no reminders to attend to this.	
		Did not initiate movement from left to right and needed constant support.	Sometimes showed control of directional movement but still needed support.	Moved left to right with minimal intervention but needed reminder to go to a new line when out of space.	Moved left to right quickly and efficiently. Moved to a new line when needed and needed no reminders.	
D O I N G	Rereading as if to seek help	Did not initiate rereading to seek help writing the next letter.	Rarely initiated rereading to seek help to write the next letter.	Sometimes initiated rereading to seek help to write the next letter.	Almost always initiated rereading to seek help to write the next letter.	
	Rereading for accuracy	Did not initiate any rereading to check the accuracy of what was written.	Rarely initiated rereading to check the accuracy of what was written.	Sometimes reread to check that the message was accurate with minimal support.	Almost always reread to check accuracy in a fast and efficient manner with no support.	
	Self-correcting	If errors were made did not notice or correct them.	If errors were made, noticed, and self-corrected on one occasion.	If errors were made, noticed, and self-corrected with some speed on most occasions.	When errors were made was fast to self-correct or wrote independently without error.	
	Fluency	Writing was slow and labored. Required high support to form letters or words.	Writing was generally slow but for known words or letters but pace picked up.	Writing was mostly fast and fluent but faltered over formation of some letters or words.	Writing was fast and fluent.	
					Total Score = ___	/ 30

Figure 1. Early Writing Observational Rubric.

Written message

The written message element of the EWOR (drawing on Halliday & Hassan, 1976; MacKenzie, Scull, & Munsie, 2013; McCutchen, 2011; and Watanbe & Hall-Kenyon, 2011) was used to rate every written message produced within the RR lesson by both groups. Using the measure, the observer rated each item along a scale of 0 to 3. There were five items and the maximum raw score in the written message element of the rubric is 15 (see Figure 2).

Reliability and validity

For the observational element, inter-rater reliability of ratings was established between three raters (the first author and two other raters). Kappa ratings ranged from $K = .62$ to $K = 1.0$. A two-way mixed consistency average that measures intra-class correlation (ICC) was also calculated to assess the degree to which coders provided consistency in their ratings of the items and ranged between .78 and 1.0 ($p > .05$). The alpha coefficient was .78. Inter-items correlations were also calculated and none were so high that one might consider they were measuring the same thing. For the written message element, Kappa ratings ranged from $\kappa = .51$ to $\kappa = .65$. An ICC was calculated and ranged between .70 and .86 ($p < .05$) and were, thus, sufficient for research purposes (Graham, Milanowski, & Miller, 2012).

In terms of validity, convergent validity was established between the OSELA's HRSW task and WV (Clay, 2013) and growth on items that considered use of letter-sound information, orthographic information, and writing vocabulary. Results demonstrated correlation between growth in use of letter-sound relationship and WV ($r = .53, p < .01$), and HRSW ($r = .33, ns$). There was also a correlation between growth in use of orthographic information and WV ($r = .43, p < .01$), and HRSW ($r = .33, ns$). Another source of validity evidence is that the assessment was sensitive to change over occasions, as reported in Results.

Results

Differences in change over time in children's use of sources of information

General changes

Differences in change over time in observed writing behaviors that would infer that children were using sources of information like oral language, orthographic or letter-sound information, and knowledge

			Written Message			
Construct	Description	Score of 0	Score of 1	Score of 2	Score of 3	Total
Legibility	Quality of Transcription*	Not legible. Uniformity of height, width, and spacing not apparent. Very large. Letters formed incorrectly	Legible in parts. Some words uniform in height, width, and spacing although large. Some letters formed correctly	Mostly legible. Height, width, and spacing between words mostly uniform. Not overly large. Letters mostly formed correctly	Completely legible. Height, width, and spacing of words appropriate and not overly large. Letters formed correctly.	
Micro-levels of language	Linguistic Complexity*/**	Message could not be considered a complete or simple sentence.	Message is a simple short sentence.	One long sentence or two or more simple short sentences.	Two or more sentences. At least one is a long sentence.	
	Linguistic Texture ***	No use of cohesive ties.	At least 1 cohesive tie.	At least 2 cohesive ties.	3 or more cohesive ties.	
	Punctuation and Capital Letters****	No capital letters or punctuation.	Capital letters or punctuation used (perhaps not appropriately).	Used capital letters and punctuation in at least one sentence.	Used capital letters and punctuation in two or more sentences.	
Macro-levels of language	Organization and message intent ****	Message is incomprehensible to the reader.	Although not organized in a logical manner message is somewhat clear to the reader.	Message is comprehensible and organized logically in one sentence.	Over 2 or more sentences child develops an idea into a coherent message.	
					Total Score	__/15

Note: Informed by ***Halliday & Hassan, 1976; *MacKenzie, Scull, & Munsie, 2013; **McCutchen, 2011; ****Watanbe & Hall-Kenyon, 2011

Record the message written (circle cohesive ties)

Figure 2. Early Writing Observational Rubric (Written message).

about how print works were considered at group level. To describe overall patterns in group change over time, measures of central tendency for first and final observations were calculated using SPSS (see Table 2). At first observation, the slow-progress group had higher mean ratings than the fast-progress group for all items except for use of letter-sound relationships and written vocabulary. An independent samples t-test demonstrated that the only difference between groups that was statistically significant was that the use of directional rules by the slow-progress group ($M = 2.88, SD = .35$) was higher than the fast-progress group's ($M = 2.17, SD = .75$) means, $t_{(12)} = 2.36, p < .05, d = 1.21$.

We examined differences between the observed writing behaviors of the slow- and fast-progress groups at the final observation. The fast-progress group had higher mean ratings for use of orthographic information, letter-sound relationships, and concept of word. The only statistically significant difference between the slow-progress group ($M = .50, SD = .55$) and the fast-progress group ($M = 1.50, SD = .55$) was in terms of observed independence in use of orthographic information, $t_{(12)} = -2.61, p < .05, d = 1.81$.

Rate of change over time

Next, we considered the difference between the rates of change over time in both groups' use of sources of information. We used hierarchical linear modeling (Raudenbush & Bryk, 2002) to estimate group rates of growth between first and final observation for all items in the Using section of the rubric and a subtotal score (the sum of the items in this section). We ran a random coefficients regression model to estimate a rate of growth over time for the Using ratings of the rubric for each group. Time was entered as a predictor variable and the resulting equation was:

$$\text{Level 1}: Y_{ti} = \pi_{01} + \pi_{1i}(\text{time}) + e_{ti}$$

$$\text{Level 2}: \pi_{01} = \beta_{00} + r_{0i}$$

$$\pi_{1i} = \pi_{1i} = \beta_{10} + r_{1i}$$

In terms of overall growth using the subtotal score, the resulting model for the rate of growth for the slow group was: rate of change over time in observed writing behaviors (Using) = 10.63 + 1.75 (time). In other words, the best estimate for the slow group's base Using subtotal score was 10.63 (out of a possible maximum of 18) and the best estimate for their rate of growth between first and last observation was 1.75, $p = .03$. In contrast, for the fast-progress group the model was: rate of change in observed writing behaviors (Using) = 9.00 + 4.33 (time). The best estimate for this rate of growth was statistically significant ($p < .05$). Essentially, the fast-progress group had a lower estimated base score with a rate of growth that was nearly 2.5 times that of the slow group.

The breadth and variability of change

To understand more about how the fast-progress group differed from the slow-progress group in use of sources of information, we compared the estimated rates of growth for each group (see Table 3) on

Table 2. Mean EWOR ratings: Slow- (n = 8) and fast- (n = 6) progress groups at first and final observation.

| | Slow-Progress Group (n = 8) | | | | Fast-Progress Group (n = 6) | | | |
| | First | | Final | | First | | Final | |
Item	M	SD	M	SD	M	SD	M	SD
Composing	1.75	0.87	2.50	0.75	1.50	0.55	2.33	0.82
Visual Information	0.63	0.52	0.87	0.35	0.50	0.55	1.50	0.55
Letter-sounds	1.13	0.35	1.38	0.52	1.16	0.41	2.00	0.53
Writing vocabulary	1.75	0.87	2.00	0.53	1.83	0.41	1.67	0.82
Concept of word	2.50	0.53	2.62	0.52	1.83	0.75	2.83	0.41
Directionality	2.88	0.35	3.00	0.00	2.17	0.75	3.00	0.00
Rereading for more information	1.25	0.71	1.38	0.52	1.16	0.41	1.50	0.55
Rereading for accuracy	0.75	0.46	0.63	0.74	0.66	0.82	1.17	0.75
Self-correcting	0.12	0.35	0.00	0.00	0.00	0.00	0.50	0.55
Fluency	6.62	2.13	2.00	0.63	7.50	2.34	2.00	0.00

Table 3. Rates of growth on EWOR for slow- (n = 8) and fast-progress groups (n = 6).

	Slow-Progress Group			Fast-Progress Group		
Item	Coefficient	t-ratio	p value	Coefficient	t-ratio	p value
		Using				
Composition	.75	2.19	ns	.83	2.97	.03
Visual information	.25	1.63	ns	1.00	4.24	.01
Letter-sounds	.25	1.06	ns	.83	2.97	.03
Writing vocabulary	.25	1.06	ns	−.16	−.45	ns
Concept of word	.13	1.06	ns	1.00	3.00	.03
Direction	.13	1.00	ns	.83	2.73	.04
Using subtotal	**.63**	**.92**	**ns**	**4.33**	**3.49**	**.01**
		Doing				
Rereading for information	0.13	0.38	ns	0.33	1.73	ns
Rereading for accuracy	−0.13	−0.45	ns	0.50	2.44	.05
Self-correction	−0.13	−1.03	ns	0.50	2.25	ns
Fluency	0.75	2.55	.03	0.83	2.71	.04
Doing subtotal	**0.63**	**0.98**	**ns**	**2.17**	**2.85**	**.04**

Note. ns = non-significant.

each item in this section of the rubric. The fast-progress group had significant rates of growth in every item except writing vocabulary.

To further describe and examine the breadth and variability of change over time between the two groups we conducted a qualitative analysis of our sources of data. The rubric ratings could be interpreted as predefined codes that described aspects of the writing process, but without analysis, they might lack meaning. To display our data, and to analyze change over time, we used an event-listing matrix for each child (Miles, Huberman, & Saldaña, 2014). Each item of the rubric formed the rows of the matrix and the columns represented time points. Miles et al. stated that this method of data display "permits a researcher to preserve the chronology of events and illuminate the processes that are occurring" (p. 194).

We displayed multiple sources of data in event-listing matrices to combine (1) descriptive statistics (the ratings in observed writing behaviors) and (2) observation notes from videos, and exemplars from the writing samples. Each cell was populated with the rubric rating and notes taken during observations. To extend description to the identification of essential features and the ways in which they interact (Glesne, 1999), we visually inspected matrices with three questions in mind: what changed, what stayed the same, and what emerged anew. We examined patterns from time-point to time-point and over the course of the intervention. We looked across each subconstruct with these three questions in mind and wrote descriptions about emerging patterns in narrative form. We annotated the matrices with symbols to illustrative a positive progression (as represented by +), a regression (as represented by -), or a new observed behavior (represented by *) in the sources of information the child used. Having described and analyzed the patterns for each child in each group, we were faced with the task of identifying the characteristics of change over time for each group in the fast- or slow-progress groups. To do this, we collapsed the data contained in the individual event listing matrices to a group matrix and analyzed this data for patterns of change over time. This analysis revealed two key areas that differentiated the fast- and slow-progress groups, namely composing and use of orthographic information.

Composing

Both the slow- and fast-progress groups were quite similar on first observation. The children in both groups needed, in general, high support to compose a message or could write a simple message with less support. By the last observation, five of the eight children in the slow-progress group and four out of six children in the fast-progress group had made a positive progression in terms of their control of language to compose a message. Where they differed was both the efficiency with which they composed their messages and the emergence of student control of topic.

The children in the slow-progress group did indicate, at times, that they did not wish to write about a certain topic. They were, however, unable (or did not have the opportunity) to steer the conversation towards something they wanted to write about. Often the teacher would suggest an alternate topic, or pursue the same topic. Take, for example, this vignette of Ethan and his teacher, during the conversation before writing on the final observation.

> Teacher: If you went fishing in the sea what would you like to catch?
> Ethan: I already wrote a story. I don't want to.
> Teacher: Listen you are doing such a good job.
> I would like to know what you would like to catch. Butterflies don't live in the sea.
> Would you catch a dinosaur?
> They don't live in the sea. What would you catch?
> Do you know something that lives in the sea?
> Oh you want to look (child picks up book).
> A snapper?
> Oh that's cool.
> Let's write a story.
> Tell me what you would say?
> Ethan: I like to catch fish in the sea.
> Teacher: I like to catch fish in the sea. Oh that's a beautiful story.
> (Week 15, Lesson 45)

In this example, although Ethan had indicated he did not want to write about the topic, his teacher persisted in talking about the topic until he finally composed a message. This demonstrated the lack of opportunity some of the slow-progress children had to pursue a topic of interest in terms of their composition.

Ownership of the message was a hallmark of the fast-progress group. We noted for teachers whose students made fast progress that, of the six observed writing events, four children changed the topic to one that they wanted to write about or had a message ready to write. Paul, a student in the fast group, exemplifies this. In the following vignette, the teacher introduces a topic but, misunderstanding the topic, Paul indicates that he would prefer to write about something different and the teacher, open to change, provides minimal support to help him reshape his composition.

> Teacher: The Billy Goats like to eat green, green grass, don't they? So they go over the bridge every day, so they always have green, green grass to eat. What are you going to eat?
> Paul: I don't like to eat-
> Teacher: You don't like to eat grass, I know.
> Paul: Yes.
> Teacher: Well what do you like to eat?
> Paul: Um.
> Teacher: What do you think we can write?
> Paul: No (inaudible) pencils. I know what - pencils to write.
> Teacher: What do you know to write?
> Paul: I have a lot of pencils in my pencil box. I work with my pencil at my house and at the school with every stuff.
> Teacher: I work with my pencils
> Paul: Every stuff
> Teacher: What? On everything you mean?
> Paul: Yes.
> Teacher: Okay, I have a lot of pencils in my pencil box. I work with my pencils at home and at school.
> Paul: And at my….. and at my house.
> (Week 17, Lesson 61)

Use of orthographic information

Children in the slow-progress group did not exhibit much change over time in use of orthographic information and this pattern of change did not vary amongst the group. Two children received a rating of 0 in the first observation and received a rating of 1 in the final observation. For all other children ($n = 6$) the ratings remained the same (a rating of 1). For example, Hailey wrote the sentence "I would go play on the monkey bars and swing off" Her teacher contributed the /ould/ in "would," the /ay/ in "play," and the /ar/ in "bars," The children in the slow-progress group were only ever observed to exhibit use of orthographic information once.

In contrast, three children in the fast-progress group made positive progress in their use of orthographic information, meaning that their ratings between first and final observation increased. For two students, the use of orthographic information emerged as a new behavior over time. For example, in the first observation Paul's teacher contributed the second /l/ in the word "will." By the final observation, Paul was observed to work competently with spelling patterns like the vowel-consonant /-e/ pattern for the word "home." One student remained the same in terms of use of orthographic information.

Similarities

Both the fast- and slow-progress groups were similar in terms of use of letter-sound information in that half of the children stayed the same in terms of observations of independently hearing and recording sounds in words, and the other half improved. We also noted little difference in the number of words written independently. Thirty-seven percent ($n = 20$) of the words in the slow group's written messages were written independently and 33% ($n = 15$) of the fast-progress group's were produced independently. By the final observation, 41% ($n = 65$) of the words in the slow group's written messages and 39% ($n = 22$) of the fast-progress group's were produced independently. By the final observation all children controlled directional movement and could space words without help.

In summary, in terms of use of sources of information, most children in this literacy intervention could control directional movement and had a good concept of word. Over time, differences emerged between the slow- and fast-progress groups, particularly in their use of orthographic information or ability to use more complex spelling patterns. This was apparent in observations of the writing events, statistically significant higher mean ratings, and a positive rate of growth in this area. In addition, the fast-progress group demonstrated a significant rate of overall growth in terms of their use of sources of information like composing, use of letter-sounds relationships, and directional rules about print. We also noted a trend towards more ownership of the composition process.

Differences in change over time in children's strategic activity inferred by observed writing behaviors

General changes

Similar to our analysis of change over time in the sources of information that children used, we first examined measures of central tendency at first and final observation of behaviors like rereading for the next word, rereading for accuracy, and self-correction. Taken together, these behaviors would infer active monitoring, searching, and cross-checking (see Table 2). We referred to this problem-solving as *doing*. We also considered children's overall fluency. Results indicated that the difference in observed self-correction between the slow-progress group ($M = .00$, $SD = .00$) and the fast-progress group ($M = .50$, $SD = .55$), was statistically significant, $t_{(12)} = -.50$, $p < .05$, for the final observation.

Rate of change over time

We used the same method of analysis (HLM) that we utilized in Research Question 1 to estimate a rate of growth for the slow- and fast-progress groups in terms of observed behaviors that would infer strategic activity. We ran a random coefficients regression model to estimate the rate of growth over time for the Doing ratings using the rubric ratings for each group. Time was entered as a predictor variable and the resulting equation was:

$$\text{Level 1}: Y_{ti} = \pi_{01} + \pi_{1i}(\text{time}) + e_{ti}$$

$$\text{Level 2}: \pi_{01} = \beta_{00} + r_{0i}$$

$$\pi_{1i} = \beta_{10} + r_{1i}$$

The model for the rate of growth for the slow group was: rate of change over time in Doing = 3.37 + .63 (time). The best estimate for the slow group's base Doing score was 3.37 (out of a possible maximum of 12) and the best estimate for their rate of growth between first and last observation was .63, $p = .39$. In contrast, for the fast-progress group the model was: rate of change in Doing = 3.00 + 2.17 (time). The best estimate for their base score was 3.00 and the best estimate for the rate of growth was 2.17, $p < .05$. Similar to their use of sources of information, the fast-progress group had lower estimated base scores but had a rate of growth that was nearly 3.5 times that of the slow group and was also statistically significant.

In terms of the rates of growth for individual items, both groups had statistically significant rates of growth in fluency (see Table 3) and the fast-progress group had a significant rate of growth in terms of rereading for accuracy. It is worth noting, however, that the rate of growth in terms of rereading for accuracy and self-correction was negative (−.13) between time points for the slow group and positive (.50) for the fast-progress group. The fast-progress group was demonstrating positive rates of growth in observed behaviors like rereading and editing, which infers they were more active in monitoring the accuracy of their written messages.

The breadth and variability of change

Next, we examined the breadth and variability of children's strategic activity inferred by observable editing behaviors like pausing, rereading, and revising. To do this we examined the data displayed in event listing matrices (Miles et al., 2014) as described previously.

Rereading for more information

We examined our data to consider change over time in rereading behaviors that might infer that children were searching for more information. This behavior was hallmarked by the children rereading their sentence or a word when they were looking to generate the next letter or the first letter of a new word. The slow group was variable in terms of their control of these behaviors. Three children regressed by the final observation, three stayed the same, and only two showed a progression. In contrast, for the fast-progress group we noted stability over time in this behavior. All children exhibited this behavior at least once at first and final observation, and three children exhibited the behavior on a few occasions by the final observation.

Rereading for accuracy

We then inspected the slow and fast group's event-listing matrices to examine how the slow- and fast-progress groups differed in terms of rereading for accuracy. Four children in the slow-progress group reread at least once to monitor the accuracy of what they had written. At the first observation four of the six children in the fast-progress group reread their sentence at least once for accuracy. For example, Courtney wrote *anb* instead of *and* she looked back, and said to the teacher "that's not right," although she could not do anything about it.

By the final observation, all but one of the fast-progress group reread at least once to monitor the accuracy of their message. In contrast, the slow-progress group again exhibited variability and limited control of this behavior. Half ($n = 4$) of the group were only observed to reread the accuracy of their message once and three children regressed by not rereading for accuracy at all.

Self-correction

Self-correction involves noticing and correcting an error independently. At the first observation, all children but one failed to notice and self-correct an error. By the final observation half ($n = 3$) of the fast-progress group were observed to notice, comment on, and fix an error. None of the children in the slow-progress group noticed, let alone fixed, an error. It seems that, as a group, the fast-progress group began to show early self-correcting behaviors. In terms of noticing or self-correcting an error, all these behaviors were related to errors at letter- and not at word-level.

Fluency

We also considered the fluency with which children transcribed the message onto the page. Children in both the slow- and fast-progress group demonstrated similar patterns of change over time, but by the end of the intervention all children's writing was mostly fast and fluent, faltering only over unknown words.

In summary, children in the fast-progress group had significant rates of growth in terms of observed behaviors like rereading what was already written for accuracy or reading in an effort to generate the next word. They also were observed to self-correct, a behavior that only occurred once in the 16 observations of the slow-progress group. This emerging behavior was restricted to noticing letter-level errors.

Differences in change over time in children's written messages

General changes

We examined overall average ratings in terms of children's ratings in terms of legibility and linguistic complexity of the written messages produced by the slow- and fast-progress groups (see Table 4). The differences in means for the fast-progress group were higher for all items, except linguistic texture which was the same as the slow-progress group. The difference between means was statistically significant for legibility, $t_{(672)}$, -2.85, $p < .05$, $d = .23$, linguistic complexity, $t_{(672)}$, -3.63, $p < .01$, $d = .28$, organization, $t_{(672)}$, -2.05, $p < .05$, $d = .1$, and overall total score, $t_{(672)}$, -2.85, $p < .05$, $d = .22$.

Change over time

Change over time in general features of children's written messages at six intervals over the course of the intervention were calculated by calculating measures of central tendency in the legibility, linguistic complexity, linguistic texture, punctuation and capitalization, and organization of their messages. The six intervals consisted of average ratings for Lessons 10, 12, and 13 (Time 1), Lessons 20, 21, and 22 (Time 2), Lessons 30, 31, and 32 (Time 3), Lessons 40, 41, and 42 (Time 4), Lessons 50, 51, and 52 (Time 5), and Lessons 60, 61, and 62 (Time 6). Our rationale for using these three lessons at these time points was that average ratings would be less likely to include error than if we chose single lessons and that the ratings would be taken at equal points in the children's programs.

To examine if differences existed between groups, we conducted an independent t-test between groups on each of the constructs at each of these points in time. This analysis revealed little. None of the differences between groups were statistically significant, except for the difference between the average mean legibility and linguistic texture ratings at Time 2. The mean legibility rating of the fast-progress group ($M = 1.94$, $SD = 0.42$) was higher than that of the slow-progress group ($M = 1.54$, $SD = 0.72$), $t_{(40)}$, -2.16, $p < .05$, $d = .68$. The mean linguistic texture rating of the low-progress group ($M = 1.95$, $SD = 0.95$) was higher than that of the fast-progress group ($M = 1.28$, $SD = 1.01$), $t_{(40)}$, 2.22, $p < .05$, $d = .68$.

Paths of change over time

We knew that the average ratings for each group, in terms of the legibility and complexity of their written messages, varied little. We wanted to consider, however, how these messages changed over time and how these progressions differed for the slow- and fast-progress groups. To do this we plotted empirical growth plots with time (by time points 1 through 6) on the x-axis and average ratings on the y-axis to visually inspect the path of change over time for each item (Singer & Willett, 2003). For the slow-progress group, we noted that average ratings ranged between one and 2.5. When ratings in micro-levels of language (linguistic complexity) rose, ratings in terms of legibility tended to dip and vice versa (see Figure 3). Message organization changed little over time.

Table 4. Mean EWOR (Written message) ratings: Slow (n = 8) and fast group (n = 6).

Item	Slow-Progress Group (n = 374)		Fast-Progress Group (n = 300)	
	M	SD	M	SD
Legibility	1.64	0.71	1.79	0.58
Linguistic complexity	1.43	0.51	1.58	0.53
Linguistic texture	1.84	0.84	1.84	0.93
Punctuation	1.80	0.46	1.88	0.48
Organization	2.00	0.30	2.03	0.30
Total Score	8.71	1.71	9.12	1.94

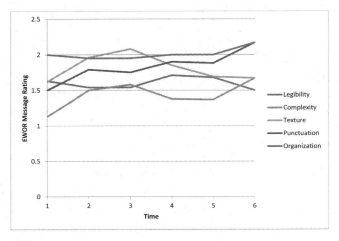

Figure 3. Path of change over time in EWOR: Written message for low-progress group ($n = 8$).

For the fast-progress group, we noted that over time ratings became more closely aligned (see Figure 4). In other words, ratings became more closely intertwined. In a similar pattern to the slow-progress group, ratings in message legibility corresponded with dips in micro-levels of language (linguistic texture). This pattern, however, dissipated halfway through the intervention.

Rates of change

We used HLM to estimate group rates of change in the linguistic complexity and legibility of children's written messages. Similar to Research Questions 1 and 2, we ran a random coefficients regression model to estimate the rate of growth over time for the written message rubric ratings for each group. Time was entered as a predictor variable and the resulting equation was:

$$\text{Level 1: } Y_{ti} = \pi_{01} + \pi_{1i} (\text{time}) + e_{ti}$$

$$\text{Level 2: } \pi_{01} = \beta_{00} + r_{0i}$$

$$\pi_{1i} = \beta_{10} + r_{1i}$$

The model for the rate of growth for the slow group was: rate of change over time in written message $= 3.37 + .63$ (time). The best estimate for the slow group's base written message ratings was 8.31 (out of a possible maximum of 15) and the best estimate for their rate of growth over the course of the intervention was .01, $p = .04$. In contrast, for the fast-progress group the model was: rate of change in

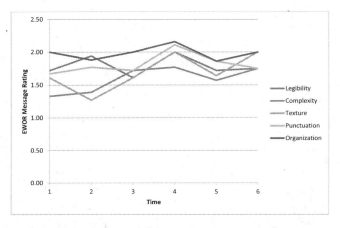

Figure 4. Path of change over time in EWOR: Written message for fast-progress group ($n = 6$).

Table 5. Rates of growth on EWOR (Written message) for slow- (n = 8) and fast- (n = 6) progress groups.

Item	Slow-Progress Group			Fast-Progress Group		
	Coefficient	t-ratio	p value	Coefficient	t-ratio	p value
Legibility	.00	0.81	ns	.00	−0.67	ns
Linguistic complexity	.00	0.58	ns	.00	2.77	.01
Linguistic texture	.00	2.82	.01	.00	0.54	ns
Punctuation	.00	3.17	ns	.00	1.46	ns
Organization	.00	1.55	ns	.00	0.15	ns
Message Total	**.01**	**1.98**	**.04**	**.01**	**1.19**	**ns**

Note. ns = non-significant.

written message = 8.88 + .01 (time). The best estimate for this rate of growth was, however, not statistically significant, $p = .09$.

We also examined each item on the rubric to consider if there were differences in terms of the rates of growth in terms of the legibility of their messages, and micro- and macro-levels of language. The results demonstrated there was little growth for either group. For both groups their rate of overall growth was a tenth of scale score per ten lessons and they exhibited flat rates of growth over time (see Table 5).

Discussion

The purpose of our study was to provide a description of the differences in change over time in the early writing development of two groups of children, identified as at risk of later literacy difficulties, who made differential progress in the context of an early literacy intervention. Specifically, we described differences between what and how children who made fast progress and those who made slow progress wrote. First, we sought to describe differences in how each group's use of sources of information while writing changed over time. Second, we described differences in how each group's observable writing behaviors (rereading as if to search for information or to monitor for accuracy, self-correction, and overall fluency) that inferred strategic actions changed over time. Third, we described differences in how the linguistic complexity and legibility of each group's written messages changed over time.

Change in use of sources of information is multi-dimensional for fast-progress writers

We examined how children's independence in composing a message, use of letter-sound relationships, use of orthographic information, use of knowledge about conventions of print, and use of a writing vocabulary changed between the beginning and end of the intervention. Our findings demonstrated that the fast-progress group had higher overall ratings at the end of the intervention, as measured by the rubric total score. This was despite the fact that the slow-progress group's ratings were higher than the fast-progress group's ratings at the start of the intervention.

The fast-progress group's rate of growth in their use of sources of information was nearly 2.5 times that of the slow group overall. When we examined rates of growth on individual items on the rubric we noted that the fast-progress group's rate of growth was positive and statistically significant in terms of their use of language to compose a message, use of letter-sound and orthographic information, and use of conventions of print. These results echo the findings of Kamberelis (2002), who concluded that change over time in observed writing behaviors was multidimensional and simultaneous. Unlike Kamberelis (2002), however, because we identified both a slow- and fast-progress group we found that this was only true for the fast-progress group.

By the end of the intervention, fast-progress writers were beginning to move beyond merely encoding simple letter-sound correspondences in their independent spelling. Moreover, this group were observed to independently use more complex spelling patterns. It makes sense that this group were then able to produce more words independently and accurately at the end of the intervention in the WV task. These finding echoes that of McGee et al. (2015) about reading because it demonstrates that children must also become adept at using the code in writing if we expect them to achieve first-grade writing benchmarks. Indeed, as Boocock et al. (1998) stated, experiencing success solving the task of writing new words would likely add, in a reciprocal manner, to children's writing vocabulary which in turn would "allow for the possibility of extending knowledge about the orthographic regularities and morphemic units across words" (p. 42). This emerging ability to use orthographic information bodes well in terms of overall literacy development, with research suggesting that orthographic awareness accounts for variance in later literacy development over and above phonological abilities (Dreyer, Luke, & Melican, 1995).

Composing, a cognitively demanding task, involves generating an idea to write and translating this message from oral to written form that can be understood by others (Galbraith, 2009). In our study, the fast-progress group, the children who produced more words at the end of the intervention, were not only better spellers, but also could compose messages in a more independent manner. They had a statistically significant rate of growth on this item, indicating that they were composing more with less teacher help and over time demonstrated flexibility to change the topic of their message. Qualitative analysis of the conversations that occurred between the teacher and child prior to writing the messages also revealed that fast-progress writers were able to change the topic of conversation and compose independently. We suggest this may be due to two factors. First, the children in the fast-progress group may have had better control of oral language. Children experiencing difficulties in oral language development face significant difficulties in the production of written texts (Dockrell & Connelly, 2015). Two, the actual process of co-constructing the message with teacher support may have been more effective. As Myhill and Jones (2009) suggested, the process of oral rehearsal and dialogue with a peer or adult can help children to compose as it gives children the opportunity to organize their thoughts and bridge the gap between thought and text. The reason is unclear and certainly warrants further analysis because it is clear that children who made slow progress were less able to change the topic of conversation and compose independently.

Revision behaviors were the hallmark of the fast-progress group

Our second research question revolved around the emergence of observable writing behaviors like rereading as if to search for more information, rereading as if to monitor the accuracy of the written message, and self-correction. Taken together these behaviors could be considered both as leading to or being directly involved in the revision process (Fitzgerald, 1987). Our results indicated that, overall, the fast-progress group had a statistically significant rate of growth that was nearly 3.5 times that of the slow-progress group in the rubric's Using subtotal scores. Although both groups had positive rates of growth for fluency, only the fast-progress group had positive rates of growth for rereading for accuracy. In fact, the slow-progress group had negative rates of growth for rereading for accuracy and self-correction. Our qualitative analysis supported these results in that the fast-progress group were observed to take steps that would lead to them potentially noticing an error (rereading), then noticing errors, and attempting to fix the error, albeit at letter rather than word level.

It seems, therefore, that similar to models of skilled writing, these actions of reviewing and revising were important and were what set the fast-progress group apart from the slow-progress group in observable writing behaviors. Clay (in Doyle, 2013) asserted that self-correction, and the problem-solving it entails, is tutorial for readers as it reinforces the processes of monitoring, searching, choosing, and evaluating and lifts the child's ability to deal with new levels of complexity (p. 642). Perhaps, in a sense, the same might be true for writing.

Little change or difference in written messages

Our third research question focused on change over time in the legibility and linguistic complexity of the children's written messages. Although overall the fast-progress group had higher ratings than the slow-progress group, there was little growth over time for either group. Essentially, both groups continued to write linguistically simple messages of one to two sentences on a daily basis. Perhaps this finding is due to the confines of time within the RR lesson. Equally, this may be all that they were expected to write and they were not supported to extend their message.

This finding in itself poses two challenges. First, in today's classrooms, children's progress is often judged solely on their written messages through the use of rubrics (e.g. Calkins, 2013). Had we judged progress solely on what was written in this study, we would have found that there was little difference between both groups. In this study, the main difference that set the slow- and fast-progress writers apart was not in what they wrote but how they wrote. This has implications for both writing assessment and instruction, particularly for children at risk of later literacy difficulties. Second, the simple messages of one or two sentences produced in this study did not resemble standards set forth by the Common Core State Standards (National Governors Association for Best Practices, 2010) for first grade. Perhaps by the end of first grade the children might be able to meet these standards.

Dips in legibility coincide with increases in micro-levels of language

By plotting change on empirical growth plots, we found that as children's messages became more linguistically complex at a micro-level (for example, by using more cohesive ties), they received lower ratings for legibility and vice versa. This finding supports the idea of development proceeding in overlapping waves (Siegler, 2006) with approaches to a task being variable before reaching stability. It also echoes Galbraith's (2009) assertion that as task demands increase, other processes may be compromised. We found that the fast-progress group seemed to coordinate ratings over time meaning that the ratings across items that considered micro- and macro-levels of language and legibility were similar. As the fast-progress group appeared to achieve more stability and integration between writing linguistically more complex messages, they simultaneously controlled lower-order transcription skills. Their approach to the task of writing was, perhaps, becoming less variable, and more integrated as posited by overlapping waves theory (Siegler, 2006).

Limitations and future directions

As with any study it is necessary to acknowledge potential limitations of our study. One limitation of our findings is that our descriptions of differences in writing development are restricted to the population we studied, one small group of struggling writers in a specific intervention. We suggest, however, that such a population was ideal for the purpose of our study. Similar to Sharp et al.'s (2008) study of spelling development, we hypothesized that by conducting our study with this population (struggling first graders), we were likely to observe a period during which rapid growth might occur. We applied stringent criteria to identify our candidates using a well established measure of early written production, the WV task from the OSELA (Clay, 2013).

We expected rapid growth because participants all started the intervention with similar ability in writing in terms of written production. In addition to this, with an intervention that has the same lesson framework for each daily lesson one would expect rapid growth over time. Thus, the participants in this study provided us with the opportunity to see development slowed down (due to the nature of their difficulties) but also accelerated (due to the nature of the intervention). Like Sharp et al. (2008) we do, however, accept that the greatest periods of change might have already occurred prior to the study, or perhaps had yet to occur. Given the definitive time span of the intervention and the use of an extant data set, we were unable to study either.

It is plausible that the nature of the writing segment of the RR lesson may have constrained development. Because the segment is short (no more than approximately ten minutes) the children were limited in what they could write. A counter argument to this might be that with increased fluency the children could and perhaps should have written more. A benefit of using the writing section of the RR lesson in this study was that message intent was free to vary because children are engaged in a conversation where they can write about a topic that interests them (cf. Clay, 2005, p. 54). In addition to this, similar instructional formats were repeated during each writing event and, indeed, between teachers. We suggest, therefore, that the benefits of studying change over time within this instructional format outweighed the disadvantage of the short time span.

An element of the study that we did not attend to was teacher instructional moves. Rather, we concentrated on describing children's writing development within an instructional context, not a controlled independent task. We did this because we were interested in the genesis of independence within this instructional context. We agree with Bergmann, Magnusson, and El-Khouri (2003) that the functioning of an individual within the situation in which development occurs permits a more nuanced and holistic understanding of development as it naturally occurs. Certainly, if we had examined change by looking at written messages only and not considering observed writing behaviors we would have learned little about the differences between groups. It is certainly plausible that variation in development could be attributed to teacher instruction, particularly in terms of conversations prior to writing, and, indeed, teacher's expectations in terms of message length. We also did not examine confounding factors like individual socioeconomic status.

We suggest that this study points towards different avenues of inquiry to build on the knowledge gained from this study. First, we suggest that it is imperative that this type of study is replicated in a kindergarten or first-grade classroom using a design similar to Clay's (1966) original research. Such a study would provide valuable information about typical and atypical development in a general education classroom. Second, understanding more about the nature of teacher instruction, instructional moves, and interactions of the teachers in this study would be useful. Third, given that our findings suggest that certain behaviors were associated with change it would be worth testing these findings empirically in an intervention study.

Conclusion

Learning to write is a complex but important element of the process of becoming literate. In this study we described the rates, paths, breadth, and variability of change over time in the writing of two groups, both identified as at risk of later literacy difficulties, who made differential progress in the context of a literacy intervention. We found that what set the groups apart was not in what they wrote but how they wrote, the sources of knowledge they drew upon, and the editing behaviors they demonstrated as they wrote. This information is important as it points towards the types of experiences and behaviors that children who beat the odds and catch up with their peers exhibited, thus pointing towards optimal instructional contexts for struggling writers (McNaughton, 2011b). Finally, although we found that change in written messages occurred in waves, little changed in the complexity of children's messages, which raises the question: Is judging progress on written products alone satisfactory?

References

Beard, R., Myhill, D., Riley, J., & Nystrand, M. (2009). *The Sage handbook of writing development*. London, UK: Sage.

Bergman, L. R., Magnusson, D., & El-Khouri, B. (2003). *Studying individual development in an inter-individual context: A person-oriented approach*. Mahwah, NJ: L. Erlbaum Associates.

Bloodgood, J. (1999). What's in a name? Children's name writing and literacy acquisition. *Reading Research Quarterly, 34*, 342–367. https://doi.org/10.1598/RRQ.34.3.5

Boocock, C., McNaughton, S., & Parr, J. (1998). The development of a self-extending system in writing. *Literacy Teaching and Learning, 3*(2), 41–58. Retrieved from http://www.earlyliteracyinfo.org/documents/pdf/doc_124.pdf

Both-de Vries, A., & Bus, A. G. (2008). Name writing: A first step to phonetic writing? Does the name have a special role in understanding the symbolic function of print? *Literacy Teaching and Learning, 17*, 37–55.

Cabell, S., Justice, L., Zucker, T., & McGinty, A. (2009). Emergent name-writing abilities of preschool-age children with language impairment. *Language, Speech & Hearing Services in Schools, 40*, 53–66. https://doi.org/10.1044/0161-1461 (2008/07-0052)

Calkins, L. (2013). *Writing pathways: Performance assessments and learning progressions, Grades K-8*. Portsmouth, NH: Heinemann.

Chanquoy, L. (2009). Revision processes. In R. Beard, D. Myhill, J. Riley, & M. Nystrand (Eds.), *The Sage handbook of writing development* (pp. 80–97). London, UK: Sage. https://doi.org/10.4135/9780857021069.n6

Chen, Z., & Siegler, R. S. (2000). Across the great divide: Bridging the gap between understanding of toddlers' and older children's thinking [Monograph]. *Monographs of the Society for Research in Child Development, 65*(2), 1–105. Retrieved from http://www.jstor.org/stable/3181574

Clay, M. M. (1966). *Emergent reading behaviors*. Unpublished doctoral dissertation. Auckland, NZ: Department of Curriculum and Pedagogy, University of Auckland.

Clay, M. M. (2001). *Change over time in children's literacy development*. Auckland, NZ: Heinemann.

Clay, M. M. (2005). *Literacy lessons designed for individuals: Part 2 teaching procedures*. Portsmouth, NH: Heinemann.

Clay, M. M. (2013). *An observation survey of early literacy achievement*. Portsmouth, NH: Heinemann.

Clay, M. M., & Cazden, C. B. (1990). A Vygotskian interpretation of reading recovery. In L. C. Moll (Ed.), *Vygotsky and education: Instructional implications and applications of socio-historical psychology* (pp. 206–222). Cambridge, UK: Cambridge University Press. https://doi.org/10.1017/CBO9781139173674.010

D'Agostino, J. V., Rodgers, E., & Mauck, S. (2017). Addressing inadequacies of the Observation Survey of Early Literacy Achievement. *Reading Research Quarterly*. Advance online publication. https://doi.org/10.1002/rrq.181.

DeFord, D. (1994). Early writing: Teachers and children in Reading Recovery. *Literacy Teaching and Learning: An International Journal of Early Literacy, 1*, 31–56.

Dockrell, J. E., & Connelly, V. (2015). The role of oral language in underpinning the text generation difficulties in children with specific language impairment. *Journal of Research in Reading, 38*(1), 18–34. https://doi.org/10.1111/j.1467-9817.2012.01550.x

Doyle, M. A. (2013). Marie M. Clay's theoretical perspective: A literacy processing theory. In D. E. Alvermann, N. Unrau, & R. B. Ruddell (Eds.), *Theoretical models and processes of reading, sixth edition* (pp. 636–656). Newark, DE: International Reading Association. https://doi.org/10.1598/0710.26

Dreyer, L. G., Luke, S. D., & Melican, E. K. (1995). Children's acquisition and retention of word spellings. *Neuropsychology and Cognition, 11*, 291–320. https://doi.org/10.1007/978-94-011-0385-5_9

Dyson, A. H. (1983). Role of oral language in early writing processes. *Research in the Teaching of English, 17*, 1–30.

Fitzgerald, J. (1987). Research on revision on writing. *Review of Educational Research, 4*, 481–506. https://doi.org/10.3102/00346543057004481

Fitzgerald, J., & Shanahan, T. (2000). Reading and writing relations and their development. *Educational Psychologist, 35*, 39–50. https://dx.doi.org/10.1207/S15326985EP3501_5

Flynn, E., Pine, K., & Lewis, C. (2006). The microgenetic method: Time for change? *The Psychologist, 19*, 152–155.

Galbraith, D. (2009). Writing what we know: Generating ideas in writing. In R. Beard, D. Myhill, J. Riley, & M. Nystrand (Eds.), *The Sage handbook of writing development* (pp. 48–64). London: Sage. https://doi.org/10.4135/9780857021069.n4

Glesne, C. (1999). *Becoming qualitative researchers: An introduction*. New York, NY: Addison Wesley-Longman.

Graham, M., Milanowski, A., & Miller, J. (2012). *Measuring and promoting inter-rater agreement of teacher and principal performance ratings*. Center for Educator Compensation Reform. Retrieved from http://files.eric.ed.gov/fulltext/ED532068.pdf

Graham, S., Bollinger, A., Booth Olson, C., D'Aoust, C., MacArthur, C., McCutchen, D., & Olinghouse, N. (2012). *Teaching elementary school students to be effective writers: A practice guide* (NCEE 2012–4058). Washington, DC: National Center for Education Evaluation and Regional Assistance, Institute of Education Sciences, U.S. Department of Education. Retrieved from http://ies.ed.gov/ncee/wwc/publications_reviews.aspx#pubsearch

Graham, S., & Hebert, M. (2012). Writing to read: A meta-analysis of the impact of writing and writing instruction on reading. *Harvard Educational Review, 81*, 710–744. https://doi.org/10.17763/haer.81.4.t2k0m13756113566

Granott, N., & Parziale, J. (2002). Microdevelopment: A process oriented perspective for studying development and learning. In N. Granott & J. Parziale (Eds.), *Microdevelopment: Transition processes in development and learning* (pp.1–30). Cambridge, UK: Cambridge University Press. https://doi.org/10.1017/cbo9780511489709.001

Halliday, M., & Hassan, R. (1976). *Cohesion in English*. London, UK: Longman.

Haney, M. R. (2002). Name writing: A window into the emergent literacy skills of young children. *Early Childhood Education Journal, 30*, 101–105. https://doi.org/10.1023/A:1021249218339

Harmey, S. (2015). *Change over time in children's co-constructed writing* (Doctoral dissertation). Columbus, OH: Department of Teaching and Learning, The Ohio State University.

Harris, P., Fitzsimmons, P., & McKenzie, B. (2004). Six words of writing, many layers of significance: An examination of writing as a social practice in an early grade classroom. *Australian Journal of Language and Literacy, 27*, 27–45. Retrieved from http://ro.uow.edu.au/era/22/

Hayes, J. R., & Berninger, V. W. (2009). Relationships between idea generation and transcription: How the act of writing shapes what children write. In R. K. Braverman, K. Lunsford, S. McLeod, S. Null, & A. S. P. Rogers (Eds.), *Traditions of writing research* (pp. 166–180). New York, NY: Taylor and Francis/Routledge.

Jones, I. (1998). Peer relationships and writing development: A microgenetic analysis. *British Journal of Educational Psychology, 68*, 229–241. https://doi.org/10.1111/j.2044-8279.1998.tb01286.x

Juel, C. (1988). Learning to read and write: A longitudinal study of 54 children from first through fourth grades. *Journal of Educational Psychology, 80*(4), 437–447. https://doi.org/10.1037/0022-0663.80.4.437

Juel, C., Griffith, P. L., & Gough, P. B. (1985). Reading and spelling strategies of first grade children. In J. A. Niles & R. Lalik (Eds.), *Issues in literacy: A research perspective* (pp. 306–309). Rochester, NY: National Reading Conference.

Kamberelis, G. (2002). Coordinating writing and reading competencies during early literacy development. *The Fifty-First Yearbook of the National Reading Conference, 51*, 227–241.

MacArthur, C., & Graham, S. (2016). Writing research from a cognitive processing perspective. In C. A. McArthur, S. Graham, & J. Fitzgerald (Eds.), *Handbook of writing research* (2nd ed., pp. 24–40). New York, NY: The Guildford Press.

MacKenzie, N. M., Scull, J., & Munsie, L. (2013). Analysing writing: The development of a tool for use in the early years of writing. *Issues in Educational Research, 23*(3), 375–393. Retrieved from http://www.iier.org.au/iier23/mackenzie.pdf.

May, H., Gray, A., Sirinides, P., Goldsworthy, H., Armijo, M., Cecile, S., & Tognatta, N. (2015). Year One results from the multisite randomized evaluation of the i3 scale-up of Reading Recovery. *American Educational Research Journal, 52*, 547–581. https://doi.org/10.3102/0002831214565788

McCutchen, D. (1996). A capacity theory of writing: Working memory in composition. *Educational Psychology Review, 8*, 299–324. https://10.1007/BF01464076

McCutchen, D. (2011). From novice to expert: Implications of language skills and writing-relevant knowledge for memory in the development of writing skill. *Journal of Writing Research, 3*, 51–68. https://doi.org/10.17239/jowr-2011.03.01.3

McGee, L. M., Kim, H., Nelson, K. S., & Fried, M. D. (2015). Change over time in first graders' strategic use of information at point of difficulty in reading. *Reading Research Quarterly, 50*, 263–291. https://doi.org/10.1002/rrq.98

McNaughton, S. (2011a). Sensitive events in literacy development. In H. Hedges, J. Parr, & S. May (Eds.), *Changing trajectories in teaching and learning* (pp. 1–14). Wellington, NZ: NZCER Press.

McNaughton, S. (2011b). Child development studies over time. In D. Lapp & D. Fisher (Eds.), *Handbook of research on teaching the English language arts* (3rd ed., pp. 400–405). New York, NY: Routledge.

Miles, M. B., Huberman, A. M., & Saldaña, J. (2014). *Qualitative data analysis: A methods sourcebook.* Thousand Oaks, CA: SAGE Publications Limited.

Myhill, D., & Jones, S. (2009). How talk becomes text: Investigating the concept of oral rehearsal in early years' classrooms. *British Journal of Educational Studies, 57*, 265–284. https://doi.org/10.1111/j.1467-8527.2009.00438.x

National Center on Response to Intervention. (2010). *Users guide to universal screening tools chart.* Washington, DC: U.S. Department of Education, Office of Special Education Programs, National Center on Response to Intervention. Retrieved from http://www.rti4success.org/observation-survey-early-literacy-achievement-reading#class

National Governors Association Center for Best Practices, Council of Chief State School Officers. (2010). *Common Core state standards.* Washington, DC: Author.

Ouellette, G., & Sénéchal, M. (2008). Pathways to literacy: A study of invented spelling in the role of learning to read. *Child Development, 79*, 899–913. https://doi.org/10.1111/j.1467-8624.2008.01166.x

Ouellette, G., & Sénéchal, M. (2017). Invented spelling in kindergarten as a predictor of reading and spelling in Grade 1: A new pathway to literacy, or just the same road, less known? *Developmental Psychology, 53*, 77–88. https://doi.org/10.1037/dev0000179

Puranik, C. S., & Lonigan, C. J. (2014). Emergent writing in preschoolers: Preliminary evidence for a theoretical framework. *Reading Research Quarterly, 49*, 453–467. https://doi.org/10.1002/rrq.79

Puranik, C. S., Lonigan, C. J., & Kim, Y. S. (2011). Contributions of emergent literacy skills to name writing, letter writing, and spelling in preschool children. *Early Childhood Research Quarterly, 26*, 465–474. https://doi.org/10.1016/j.ecresq.2011.03.002

Raudenbush, S. W., & Bryk, A. S. (2002). *Hierarchical linear models: Applications and data analysis methods.* Thousand Oaks, CA: Sage Publications.

Rittle-Johnson, B., & Siegler, R. S. (1999). Learning to spell: Variability, choice, and change in children's strategy use. *Child Development, 70*, 332–348. https://doi.org/10.1111/1467-8624.00025

Sharp, A. C., Sinatra, G. M., & Reynolds, R. E. (2008). The development of children's orthographic knowledge: A microgenetic perspective. *Reading Research Quarterly, 43*, 206–226. https://doi.org/10.1598/RRQ.43.3.1

Siegler, R. S. (1996). *The process of change in children's thinking.* New York, NY: Oxford University Press.

Siegler, R. S. (2006). Microgenetic analysis of learning. In D. Kuhn, R. S. Siegler, & W. Damon (Eds.), *Handbook of child psychology: Volume 2* (pp. 464–509). Hoboken, NJ: John Wiley & Sons.

Singer, J., & Willett, J. (2003). *Applied longitudinal data analysis: Modeling change and event occurrence.* New York, NY: Oxford University Press.

Suggate, S., Pufke, E., & Stoeger, H. (2016). The effect of fine and grapho-motor skill demands on preschoolers' decoding skill. *Journal of Experimental Child Psychology, 141*, 34–48. https://doi.org/10.1016/j.jecp.2015.07.012

Tolchinsky, L. (2016). From text to language and back: The emergence of written language. In C. A. McArthur, S. Graham, & J. Fitzgerald (Eds.), *Handbook of writing research* (2nd ed., pp. 144–159). New York, NY: The Guildford Press.

Vellutino, F. R., Scanlon, D. M., Sipay, E. R., Small, S. G., Pratt, A., Chen, R. S., & Denckla, M. B. (1996). Cognitive profiles of difficult to remediate and readily remediated poor readers: Early intervention as a vehicle for distinguishing between cognitive and experiential deficits as basic causes of specific reading disability. *Journal of Educational Psychology, 88*, 601–638. https://doi.org/10.1037/0022-0663.88.4.601

Wagner, R., Puranik, C. S., Foorman, B., Foster, E., Wilson, L. G., Tschinkel, E., & Kantor, P. T. (2011). Modeling the development of written language. *Reading and Writing, 24*, 203–220. https://doi.org/10.1007/s11145-010-9266-7

Watanbe, L. M., & Hall-Kenyon, K. M. (2011). Improving young children's writing: The influence of story structure on kindergartners' writing complexity. *Literacy Research and Instruction, 50*, 272–293. 10.1080/19388071.2010.514035

Yaden, D. B., & Tardibuono, J. M. (2004). The emergent writing development of urban Latino preschoolers: Developmental perspectives and instructional environments for second-language learners. *Reading and Writing Quarterly, 20*, 29–61. https://doi.org/10.1080/10573560490242723

Index

Note: **Boldface** page numbers refer to tables & *italic* page numbers refer to figures.

Baker, S. 12
Ball, D. 12, 15, 25
British Ability Scales Word Reading Test II (BAS-II) 66, 67

challenges, motivation 49–50
Chard, D. 12
children: letter identification 41; literacy 29, 31, 33, 42; reading difficulties 29
children's strategic activity 87; breadth and variability of change 88; fluency 88–9; general changes 87; rate of change over time 87–8; rereading for accuracy 88; rereading for more information 88; self-correction 88
children's use, sources of information 83; breadth and variability of change 84–5, **85**; composing 85–6; general changes 83–4, **84**; orthographic information 86–7; rates of change over time 84; similarities 87
Clay, Marie 8, 16, 22, 25, 26, 30, 61, 64, 65
Coburn, C. E. 10, 11, 23
codes, Reading Recovery 5–6
Cohen, C. 12, 15, 25
collaborations, motivation 50
Common Core State Standards movement 7
community 62
comprehensive school-reform models 10
Consortium for Policy Research in Education (CPRE) 18, 19, 22
convergent learning 4

D'Agostino, J. V. 23, 24
Datnow, A. 10–12, 23, 25
Daviss, B. 12
depth, Coburn's concept of scale 11
Descubriendo la Lectura 16
dimensions of motivation 49; challenge 49–50; collaborations 50; self-efficacy 50; student interest 49

'disappearing difference' 23
divergent learning 4

early writing development of children 76–7; characterizing 77–8; data sources 81; differences in 78–9; Early Writing Observational Rubric 81–3, *82*; fast-progress writers 91–2; limitations and future directions 93–4; measuring 78; microgenetic design method 79–80; micro-levels of language 93; Observation Survey of Early Literacy Achievement 81; present study 78; promoting 77; Reading Recovery lessons 79; reliability and validity 83; sources of information 83–7; strategic activity by writing behaviors 87–9; students 80, **80**; teachers 81; written messages 89–93
Early Writing Observational Rubric (EWOR) 81, *82*; doing rubric of 82; using rubric of 82; written message element of 83, *83*
education: policy and research 10; scaling an innovation in 10–11; system 12
Elementary and Secondary Education Act 7
Elmore, R. F. 11
encoding 35, 38, 40–1
engagement theory 48
enterprise, Reading Recovery 2
epistemic community framework 1, 4–5
evidence-based reform movement 7, 10, 60, 61
EWOR *see* Early Writing Observational Rubric
expectancy-value theory of motivation 48, 52

fast-progress writers: revision behaviors 92; sources of information 91–2
first grade 47–8
Follow-Up Survey reports 24
Fullan, M. 12, 13, 25

Gersten, R. 12
Guskey, T. R. 12, 23

Hearing and Recording Sounds in Words (HRSW) 81

INDEX

hierarchical linear modeling (HLM) 35–6, 40; for level 2 predictors **39**
HRSW *see* Hearing and Recording Sounds in Words

instructional intervention, Reading Recovery 3
instructional practice 12
intensive literacy intervention 13
internal reform 11
International Reading Recovery Trainer Organization 33
Intervéntion Preventive en Lecture-écriture 16
i3 teacher attrition **20**

job-embedded professional development 14

learning systems 3–4
letter identification 30, 37–8, 41
Leveled Literacy Intervention (LLI) 22
literacy: achievement **37**, 39–40; domains 31–2, 36, *37*; interventions 29, 30, 33; learning 29, 31, 32; processing theory 82
Literacy Out Loud 52
LLI *see* Leveled Literacy Intervention
long-term reading difficulties 29

Madden, N. 11, 12
Matthew Effect 47
McDonald, S. K. 11, 19, 20
Me and My Reading Profile (MMRP) 52, **53**
MEAP *see* Michigan Education Assessment Program
meta-analysis, of reading recovery: data analysis 35–6; data sources 33–5; different literacy domains 31–2; encoding and phonological encoding 35, 38, 40–1; explicit code instruction 31; hierarchical linear modeling results **39**; literacy achievement **37**, 41; literacy domain *37*; long-term reading difficulties 29; moderate effect of 36–9; OSELA *vs.* external measures 32; purpose of study 33; quasi-experimental *vs.* experimental 38; students' literacy achievement 39–40; study design 32; sustainability 32–3; *t*-test 36; United States *vs.* other countries 33
Michigan Education Assessment Program (MEAP) 69, 71, *72*, 73
micro-levels of language, legibility coincide with 93
MMRP *see* Me and My Reading Profile
motivation levels, Reading Recovery and 47; analytic procedures 53–4; dimensions of motivation 49–50; measures 52–3, **53**; participants 51–2; pre- and post- achievement 51, *54*; research on motivation 50–1; results 54–5; structural equation modeling 53–6, *56*; teachers 57; theoretical frameworks 48–9; treatment effect on achievement 56–7
Motivation to Read Profile (MRP) 51

National Center for Response to Intervention (NCRTI) 13, 81
National Diffusion Network (NDN) 17
NCRTI *see* National Center for Response to Intervention
non Observation Survey of Early Literacy Achievement (non-OSELA) 30
North American Trainer Group 15

An Observation Survey of Early Literacy Achievement (Clay) 13
Observation Survey of Early Literacy Achievement (OSELA) 30, 47–8, 52, 53, 64, 66, 67, 69, 73, 79–81; *vs.* external measures 32; pretest scores **70**
Office of the Inspector General (OIG) 17, 18
The Ohio State University 1, 2, 15, 18, 61
OSELA *see* Observation Survey of Early Literacy Achievement

Peer-Assisted Learning Strategies 23
Petroski, H. 13
phonological awareness 31, 41
phonological encoding 35, 38, 40–1
policy initiatives 1–2
problem-solving actions 78
professional development: network of support 15; teacher-leader training 14; three-tiered job-embedded 14; training and 14
professionalism 62
programs, Reading Recovery 2–3

Reading First funding 18
Reading Recovery Council of North America (RRCNA) 15
Reading Recovery's design: face-to-face training 15; implementation pattern, features of **19–21**, 19–23; instructional format and materials for teaching children 14; mechanism for redesigning 15–16; network of professional support 15; one-to-one feature of 15; overview 13; published standards 15; regional teacher-training site 15; research and evaluation system 14; summary 16; three-tiered job-embedded professional development 14
regional teacher-training site 15
response-to-intervention (RTI) approach 21
Rodgers, E. 23, 24
royalty-free license 15
RRCNA *see* Reading Recovery Council of North America
Running Records (Clay) 22

scaffolding 49
scale-up, pitfalls of 60–1
scaling an innovation 10–11; Coburn, C. E. 11; Daviss, B. 12; features of 19; McDonald, S. K. 11, 19, 20; Schneider, B. 11, 19, 20; success and failure of 11–13; Wilson, K. G. 12; *see also* Reading Recovery's design

INDEX

Schneider, B. 11, 19, 20
school improvement networks 2–3
self-efficacy and perceived competence 50
SEM *see* structural equation modeling
shift, Coburn's concept of scale 11
skilled reading 31
Slavin, R. 11, 12
Slosson Oral Reading Test—R 64
sociocultural theory 48–9
spread, Coburn's concept of scale 11
Standards and Guidelines of Reading Recovery in the United States, 6th edition 15
Stringfield, S. 10–12, 23, 25
structural equation modeling (SEM) 51, 53, 55–6
Success for All (SFA) model 11
sustainability, Coburn's concept of scale 11
sustained effects of Reading Recovery 64; ANCOVA test results 70, **71**; classification and statistical analyses 69–70; goals of 67–8; intervention 73–4; limitation with 66–7; MANCOVA test results 70, **71**; measures 69; participants 68; prior research on 65–7; studying longer-term 66, 72
synergistic learning 4

teacher-leader training 14
teachers, Reading Recovery 57
teacher–student collaboration 50
theory, Reading Recovery 5
three-tiered job-embedded professional development 14
tools, Reading Recovery 6–7

UK National Curriculum (NC) assessment 67
United States: exponential expansion (1985–2000) 17, **17**; ideas and norms for practice 21; implementation **16**, 16–17, 25; steady decline (2000–2010) 17–18, **18**; targeted expansion (2010–2015) 18–19, **19**; *vs.* other countries 33

Vellutino, F. R. 22

Watson, Barbara 16
What Works Clearinghouse (WWC) 19, 20, **20**, 30–2, 34, 40–1
Wilson, K. G. 12
Word Reading and Phonics Skills (WRAPS) 66, 67
writing behaviors 82
Writing Vocabulary (WV) 80, 91
written messages, children's 89; change over time 89; general changes 89; legibility and linguistic complexity of 92–3; paths of change over time 89–90, *90*; rates of change 90–1, **91**
WV *see* Writing Vocabulary
WWC *see* What Works Clearinghouse